Writing and Imagery

D0493541

Aber Creative writing Guides

The Business of Writing
The Craft of Fiction
Ghost Writing
Writing Crime Fiction
Kate Walker's 12 Point Guide to Writing Romance
Writing Historical Fiction
Writing How-to Articles and Books
Writing TV Scripts
Starting to Write
Writing Soap
Writing Science Fiction
Writing and Imagery

Aber Self-Help

Choose Happiness: Ten Steps to Put the Magic Back into your Life
Write yourself well: How writing therapy can help to cure emotional
and physical pain

Aber Money Management

Understanding the numbers: the first steps in managing your money
Back to the Black: How to get out of Debt and Stay out of Debt

Aber publishing

Helping Writers Write

Writing and Imagery

How to deepen Creativity and Improve your Writing

A.J. Palmer

www.studymates.co.uk

Dedication

*To my students: each and every one of them. You made
the journey – and this book – possible.*

Reader Note:
Throughout this book the author has spelt the word holistic as *wholistic**. This is quite deliberate to reinforce the idea of the wholeness of this type of thinking and creativity.

NOTE: The material contained in this book is set out in good faith for general guidance and no liability can be accepted for loss or expense incurred as a result of relying in particular circumstances on statements made in this book. Laws and regulations are complex and liable to change and readers should check the current position with the relevant authorities where appropriate. Neither the author nor the publishers nor any/all of their agents can be held responsible for outcomes that result from actions taken by readers as a result of reading this book.

Contents

9   Visualisation   85

10   Metaphor   99

11   More on metaphor   113

12   The language and teaching of Creative Writing   127

About the Author

A. J. Palmer has three careers:

- as a writer,
- as a teacher of Creative writing, and
- as a teacher of horse-riding.

She jokes about only managing to teach two 'R's' - *writing and riding* - rather than the traditional three.

Whilst working as an equestrian photo-journalist for ten years, Ann found an initial dovetailing of two of her major passions, and was published in the U.S., New Zealand, Australia and U.K. She subsequently published romantic novels, children's fantasy stories and poetry. As a young writer testing her abilities, she published articles in women's magazines, the *Guardian*, and *Times Educational Supplement*; wrote a musical play performed in middle schools in the U.K., and was commissioned by the Jersey Wildlife Preservation Trust to write a series of stories for their Education Pack.

When Ann started writing, Creative writing was not taught in the U.K. at any level except Adult Education. So Ann bought twenty books from the States to assist her early teaching at four colleges in the West Midlands. By the time she moved away from the West Midlands, she was being head-hunted to run 3 year courses in Creative writing.

One year at Swanwick Writers Summer School, Ann ran a double workshop in Confidence which was so successful she was encouraged to fully investigate the areas of Accelerated Learning, creativity and right brain methods generally. This book is the result of those many forays with students into what was, for her at the time, unknown territory.

My grateful thanks to Julie Roxburgh for her wonderful artwork for this book.
A. J. Palmer

Foreword

As a left-hander, I have always been in my right mind. I have a natural inclination to be creative, imaginative and, some would say, 'away with the fairies'. Living in a left brain world, however, has pulled me from my natural habitat and forced me to adopt alternative ways of thinking, processing and behaving. My compulsory education taught me to think logically and analytically; organising life into lists and bullet points in the traditional 'parts-to-whole' conceit of left brain thinkers. My work was neat, orderly and double-underlined. I did not doodle on my books, nor colour outside the lines. My left brain learning got me exam results, but it did not achieve understanding. It did not fulfil my potential.

I left school for university and spent a further twelve years in higher education. Strange things began to happen: lectures in which I took notes made less sense than lectures in which I drew doodles; essays that I planned with notes and lists got lower marks than essays that were pulled together from doodles and intuition. I started to experiment and play with convention. The more I played, the more insight I gained into my studies. I had freed my mind of its left brain constraints and was thrilled with the work I could generate from my recovered *wholistic** thinking.

During my PhD, I began using images to help me plan my thesis. Being able to see the whole picture was crucial to my understanding and so I decided to draw the whole picture – literally. My plans became an A1 drawing which contained all the elements of my thesis. I could now see it all and allow it to inspire my imagination. I had no idea what I was doing – I only knew that it worked.

Shortly after I took up my crayons, I attended a confidence workshop run by Ann Palmer. Synchronicity leapt into play as I learnt about the importance of facilitating right brain thinking and using imagery to generate creativity and understanding. Suddenly I understood what I was doing and why it made sense. My confidence soared with the possibilities of enhancing my right brain activity and tapping into its infinite resources as a creative writer.

Of course, one does not have to be a creative writer to benefit from image-making. Like many people, I keep a journal. My journal, however, is littered with images and doodles. Sometimes, especially if I am emotional, drawing at random may throw up the answer to my discontent. In fact, I think I can safely say 'always' rather than 'sometimes' for the interpretation has never yet failed to shed some light on my feelings, even if that interpretation is not something I can put into words.

In the years since that first workshop, I have attended further courses with Ann and expanded my understanding and belief in right brain thinking. With practice comes a faith in your drawings – in their content rather than their artistry – and with that faith comes boundless layers of interpretation. You do not have to be an artist to use this process, which looks for meaning not artistic merit. An image is a success if it 'speaks' to you; something which is in no way dependent on its ability to fill a space at an art gallery.

As well as exploring my own right brain images, I have also been privileged to see others find meaning from drawings. Watching someone discover a hidden thought or concept from something they have produced themselves can be an intense and often exhilarating experience. Indeed, I know many, including myself, go on to hang their pictures in a prominent place to continue to inspire them long after the workshop has ended.

Sharing the potential of right brain imagery with other writers through this book is most exciting. There are few writing handbooks that can fuel your writing the way your imagination will when let loose though image interpretation. It is a gift you have always had, but may not have opened. So go on, open it...

Dr Xanthe Wells
has a PhD in Creative and Critical Writing and provides coaching and editing support to writers across a variety of disciplines, including popular fiction and business coaching. Her own writing spans from children's picture books to literary fiction and philosophy. Xanthe was Vice- Chairman of the Writers Summer School (2008-2009).

1   Why Writers Need Imagery

It is likely that, in the beginning was the IMAGE, not the word at all. Sacrilegious it may appear, but the Big Bang, evolution, and scientific knowledge all suggest the image preceded the word. Closer to home, a baby's first attempts to learn and make sense of the world are centred on images; focusing on them and sorting out the important, significant and meaningful.

This book takes a brain-based approach to the creative process. It's about the importance of imagery to writers, all writers. It does not matter what kind of writer you are or aspire to be, from hobbyist to best-selling author. Images and imagework form the basis of creative endeavour, and this book explains why this is so.

My career teaching Creative writing to adults and children gave me a lifetime to explore this subject. I learned the central role of imagery and imagework to the process and methodology of being a published writer in various genres and its value to students starting writing careers. As a colour-blind non-artist myself, I experienced much early resistance to using imagery in my personal writing projects. The reasons I now wholeheartedly champion imagery as integral to the writing process are revealed in this book.

Before looking at the core subject matter of this book – linking the creative Right Brain's attributes to key writing skills – three things need to be in place.

These are:

- establish the necessity to work with, rather than against, how the human brain is structured and functions.
- consider our dreams as personal proof, a way to validate, Right Brain I.D.
- Learn simple ways – doodling, stylised artwork – to draw out personal imagery and kickstart the creative process.

The ten key writer-skills sourced through imagery are:

1. Visualisation – the 'show, don't tell' advice.
2. Metaphor – its direct incorporation to significantly deepen the writing.
3. Dialoguing - the necessary interrogation of image for development.
4. Focus and clarity – to guarantee the reader fully comprehends your meaning.
5. Sense-based writing – to give the empathetic writer-reader contact.
6. Emotion – to ensure the reader a vicarious experience.
7. Intuition – for the unexpected and deeper insights into an original idea.
8. Imagination – kickstarted by asking 'what if'?
9. Blue sky thinking – brainstorming to expand ideas.
10. Synthesis – integration of ideas producing a variety of possible structures.

These ten key writer-skills carry a sense of coming full circle. The visualisation that produces a single image is the same one that, if patiently interrogated, will yield the overview representing a full integration of ideas. The original image needs to be imbued with a sense-based appreciation and then given time for focus and clarity to emerge. The brainstorming treatment encourages emotion, intuition and imagination to flow at their height. This accurately describes the general working of creative process.

These ten image-based attributes of our Right Brains operate simultaneously so reflect its multi-tasking nature. It's inevitable these attributes overflow into one another, have 'leaky margins'. In a real sense they feed on and off each other in the enthusiasm, personal liberation, high energy and exuberance that creative work engenders. Other common expressions that refer to imagework are 'organic' and/or *wholistic** learning. These are legitimate ways of appreciating the quantum levels of the brain that become available to the writer who wants to deepen and expand personal creativity.

2 Writing & Imagery

This chapter begins with objections because objections are the most likely reaction of a person who has not heard of the use of Right Brain methods or imagery as being an integral part of writing process.

Instead of dismissing it as 'a current fad', we start by treating resistance to the use of imagery as a potential block to creative progress. Finally we will examine the impact of education and culture as blocks to progress in using imagery in writing and see why it has taken until the 21st century for imagery to lead in the writing process.

If you have ever had the experience of saying 'I can't keep up with my thoughts, they are coming too quickly', you have connected with the Right Brain's power.

The important point to remember is the key benefit of Right Brain initiated imagework is it accesses a wider field of the mind.

Writer Tip
'Right Brain' and 'Imagery' are terms used interchangeably because the 'language' of the Right Brain is pictures, not words.

How blocks become stepping stones

Writing blocks, and creative blocks generally are viewed as 'objects', objects to be negotiated. Anything can act as a block, until the writer finds a new way of seeing which works for her or him, and develops the ability to transform the perceived stumbling block into a stepping-stone.

Here is a typical dialogue incorporating the more obvious objections to using imagery as part of writing process, followed by statements to counter those objections.

'I don't have enough writing time as it is! It'll hold up the process even more if I have to draw first!'

But using imagery in writing or imagework, as it is known, is itself a fast track that will save you time and improve your writing. You may have heard the expression 'a picture says 1,000 words'. Some people believe an image says 10, 000 words. Clearly, this is a highly empowering strategy for any writer. The act of drawing an image, takes the mind into its quantum, rather than its linear mode. It will take you ten minutes to do a

Writer Tip
Imagework involves the drawing, development and interpretation of personal images.

quick drawing, a much shorter time than it takes to rough out a 1000 word first draft.

'I want to learn to write, not draw! If I wanted to learn to draw, I'd go to an art class!'

That sounds so logical, doesn't it? It takes a while before you automatically recall we are talking another way of comprehension altogether; one sourced in an image, not in words, thoughts, ideas or concepts.

The point is that by drawing, you are using a different part of your brain – the right side - to create the image and this enhances your thinking because both sides of your brain are active, simultaneously.

When comparing Right Brain creative with Left Brain logical, we change learning methods. Left Brain is incremental, Right Brain is exponential.

It's like the move to using broadband on the internet. At the developmental level of writing process, the methodology of imagework is technically superior to any word-led exercise.

Words, sentences, paragraphs, develop linearly, one thing at a time, sequentially down the page. Images come from a different area of our brains where simultaneous multidimensionality rules. Instead of working with just one thing, ten are on offer, all at the same time, all interactive with each other. This is why writers in highly creative states exclaim... 'I can't keep up with my thoughts, they are coming too quickly!'

'I feel under confident enough about writing and having to read it out! And now you expect me to draw and share my drawings with everyone!'

You were happy to draw as a child. Maybe you even loved it. Till you discovered you weren't a Michelangelo. At a deeper level, drawing tends to concretise the abstract and make subsequent writing more accessible to the average reader. Drawing is especially helpful to those with an over-intellectualised mindset.

'What d'you mean, an over-intellectualised mindset?'

Research has revealed 80% of westerners have a Left Brain bias. A Left Brain bias means your creativity, which is Right Brain sourced, is suppressed. Your own creativity isn't available to you because of your education and training which automatically values Left Brain tasks over Right Brain ones. If you say things like 'I'm not imaginative' it's an indication of underuse of the Right Brain. The Right Brain activity of drawing helps rebalance the brain. That's a bonus.

'Drawing is for primary kids! I did this as a five year old!'

That's no bad thing. To reclaim the childlike fun in ourselves can lead to writing humorously. Humour sells. Laughter is the best medicine.

'Name some authors who use imagery as part of their writing process.'

Authors aren't usually self-revelatory about creative process. Certainly J.K. Rowling uses drawings.

'Don't you think we should focus on writing itself? I mean, there is so much to learn about technique, genre, markets, the right attitude for success.'

Again, this is such a logical approach. The counter-argument is... 'Restrict yourself to your Left Brain and you will not access your full potential as a writer.' This is because you are automatically favouring the part of your mind not designed to do creative work.

'Are you saying all writers use imagery as part of writing process?'

No. I'm saying not using imagery makes the learning process longer and unnecessarily difficult for many people who erroneously conclude they aren't creative. When the truth is they have never exercised their creative muscle. By learning image-speak you give yourself the best chance.

'I can't draw.'

Me neither. See Chapter Seven

'I'm colour blind.'

Me too. It's not important. What is important is the power of the self-generated image, the subject of the last section of this chapter.

If imagework is such an important and integral part of writing process, one very obvious question is:

Why is it only now, in the 21st century, that imagework is being incorporated in creative writing courses?

Consider the history of Creative writing over the last 25 years. We need to look at the status of the subject, and how

> **Writer Tip**
> Image-speak is the 'language' of the creative Right Brain. It is the only language of the Right Brain, and relies on the interpretive skills of the Left Brain to make sense.

that has changed. This prepares the way for understanding the rise of interest in imagework within a writing context.

Effect of a cultural shift in attitudes towards writing

In the past, writers often avoided talking about writing process altogether. Naturally, this reticence led to conjecture. Did writers have a secret formula they wanted to protect?

Today, a greater honesty and openness of attitude linked to the present status of Creative writing as an established university discipline has brought about a very different understanding.

Creative process is chaotic, messy, containing hundreds of surprises and unexpected developments which align naturally with Right Brain creative functioning.

An open attitude means the modern writer has moved from the position of not wanting or being able to talk about process to its opposite. To explore nuances of creativity in as many ways as can be devised frees the mind, raises personal energies, and encourages further creativity.

Creative writing as a university discipline

The status of Creative writing as a university discipline open to development to doctoral level has had three major effects.

1   The stamp of academic credibility validates the subject.
2   The links with university subjects provides great growth areas for future research.
3   The methodologies of all related subjects become available to the student of Creative writing. This guarantees reflexive thinking, designed to reveal improved appreciations through the use of contexts and frameworks.

The academic acceptance of Creative writing in the U.K. in the period between 1985 and 2010 has raised and expanded the status of this subject.

Students' attitudinal change

Students' attitudes towards me, as a Creative writing teacher, also subtly changed over this 25 year period. Initially, students regarded me as the person who 'gave them permission to write'. This was at the time when the subject of Creative writing was taught as a single subject at two U.K. universities. In the middle phase, students stated their major need was 'more confidence'. Latterly, students ask for ways into 'greater creativity'.

Even over as short a period as 25 years, Creative writing students mirror this cultural shift in wider society. Occasionally, when American students join a Creative writing class of British writers, their attitude is strikingly different. Again, this reflects the fact that in America, Creative writing was taught at university level several decades before it happened in the U.K. The Americans displayed an acceptance of themselves as budding writers, showed a natural confidence and unselfconsciousness in enjoying and sharing their writing. This attitude singled them out and made me, as a teacher, more aware of the habitual self-denigrating attitude of the average U.K. student when it came to talking about creativity within their writing.

A positive attitude is a key factor in effective learning. The need of permission to write reflects a person unsure whether or not it's O.K. to write.

The 'more confidence wanted' issue might simply be a self-esteem requirement but it also marked a time of transition in the status of creative writing as a subject. As the status of creative writing increased, the students' attitude changed yet again. Now they asked for ways into greater creativity.

The effect of a cultural shift in writer-attitudes towards imagework

Another societal shift has occurred over those 25 years. This shift is towards using icons and images as a fast track, a shorthand way of communicating. This extends to communicating subliminally in a fast-paced society geared to commercialism. The power of the image or icon is well-documented. By subliminal I mean the emotional affect an image and its associations can have on a person's behaviour, turning the product into a 'must-have'. This happens below the level of consciousness.

The new writer & imagery

Cultural background is hardwired into the brain as we grow.

It's that cultural background which makes one generation of people different to the next one. Without even realising it, we accept this cultural background as the basis of our lives. It becomes the norm.

Evidence from education supporting Right Brain learning methods

Writer Tip
For writers, as well as a refresh, reframing is an ideal way of thinking about using the same material to fit specific writing markets.

The present young generation is highly image-literate. This shift to image as major societal communicator, backed and supported by a sophisticated technology, removes many barriers to doing imagework as part of writing process.

Certain leading educationalists, such as Sir Ken Robinson, maintain that the present educational system, being a Left Brain biased one, stifles the development of creativity in young people. Sir Ken champions Right Brain methods as a way to rectify this imbalance. Other educational systems favouring Right Brain methods have become popular in recent years.

* E.g. neurolinguistic programming–with the acronym N.L.P. This system is useful to writers in two specific ways. N.L.P. advocates trying new methods and has the remit of recontextualisation, commonly called reframing.

* Accelerated Learning, a student-centred rather than a teacher-centred method of learning. In Accelerated Learning workshops, students take on far greater responsibility for their own learning than conventionally.

Students are motivated to take on more responsibility because the tasks set in Accelerated Learning workshops are sufficiently challenging, with a playful element and high interactive content. Accelerated Learning practitioners claim their methods are 300% more effective than conventional educational methods.

As writers, the outcome is to see imagery as an integral part of writing process: a natural, normal and highly appropriate activity.

Why wasn't the link between writing and imagery established sooner?

For a long time in the academic world, differing subject-areas had little to do with each other. It was taboo to cross 'disciplinary lines'.

Superficially, writing and drawing have little in common. They use different tools, pen and brush. Writing is black and white, drawing is colour. Unless you live in a society which uses a pictorial language, like Egyptian, or a symbolic one, like Chinese, the links between text-making and image-making are far from apparent.

The self-generated Image

We can all understand a picture of a dog as a two dimensional representation of a familiar domestic animal. However, the number of different words used to describe this familiar animal equal the number of languages existent on the planet.

This same proliferation of outer images can make us lazy about producing our own. We take an outer one rather than seek an inner more meaningful one. Outer images are called 'accultured images' - the ones offered by the culture.

Accultured images v. personal images

When writers first start doing imagework, they may produce highly accultured images. Only later, after practice and experimentation, do writers produce unique individualised images which have meaning and significance to them. As with writing a first draft, early imagework may be superficial, and generally have the *feel* - not look - of being a first attempt. i.e. a first attempt to access meaning.

Important meaning of a self-generated image

Remind yourself that you are not producing an image for an artistic purpose, but for its creative and enriching input into your writing task or project.

Key Understanding

The word 'education' is derived from the Latin 'educare' which literally means 'drawing out'. You can only draw out what is already in there. To access Right Brain knowledge we need to learn our own personal image-speak.

Right Brain input can include any or any combination of ten key writer-skills, depending on what information, perceptions and appreciations you wish to discover - or draw out - from your self-generated image.

The Ten Key Right Brain Writer Skills

1 *Visualisation* always acts as a reminder to '*show, not tell*'.

2 *Metaphor* as an encapsulation of an idea or project at the symbolic level.

3 *Dialoguing* as a way to become interactive with a self-generated image. Any question or realisation that occurs whilst drawing or contemplating the image will forward and deepen your understanding.

4 *Focus and clarity.* Specific lines of the image, especially those that don't conform to any expectation of representational art, offer a way into allowing the image to communicate its real meaning.

5 *Sense-based writing.* This involves considering how your style of drawing may translate into the range of sensory perceptions. Smell, taste, touch, hearing.

6 *Emotion.* How does your drawing make you feel? What's the emotion conveyed to you?

7 *Intuition.* These are the surprises. Your intuition at work is found in the surprises. The things you drew 'for no reason', because you just felt like it, on a whim, in a freespirited mood or moment. Remember the surprises contain meaning and a significance, though neither may be immediately obvious or available to you. A good plan is to come back to the image next day and you may well find the answer 'just comes to you'. At this point you have important evidence - a validation - you are working with your brain's natural functioning. You are learning to trust your intuition.

8 *Imagination.* As you begin to draw, stay open-minded. It will give your imagination the best chance.

9 *Blue sky thinking.* This is a deliberate extension of imagination. You invite it when co-operating with rather than rejecting the chaos that is part of Right Brain creativity in a quest for a more powerful image.

10 *Synthesis.* This is the all-in-one image that integrates the whole so the relationships between the different parts are revealed.

Ways into Imagework
Follow the methods of genius

Albert Einstein claimed his primary creative thinking took place through visual imagery and stated 'I very rarely think in words at all'. It could be said that it is primarily the image and imagination that guides the innovator to new discoveries. Writers who wish to be more creative need to learn personal image-speak.

It's easy to become interactive with images. It feels simple because, mentally, it is a movement towards an earlier form of relating to the world. Around 12-years old, the young human makes the transition to understanding concepts rather than processing reality through a series of images. Even just thinking about inner images starts the interaction.

The observer in your mind

To become 'an observer in your own mind' is zen-like. It invites you to detach from the close identification with the activities, thoughts and emotions which characterise your habitual focus. This detachment is of itself therapeutic, a short break from the demands of life. It's an opportunity to reflect and centres on the part inner images currently play in life.

Way 1 - Reality-related images

Reality-related images are familiar ones concerned with the ongoing business of daily life.
For example:

*   Imagining your child sitting an examination.
*   Visualising a husband, wife or partner at a tough interview.
*   Considering what to wear at a forthcoming party.

Now, become aware whether the event – examination, interview, party, came to your mind first as a concept or idea, or as an image. Perhaps it's a mixture? A lightning image followed by a stream of thoughts. Is it easier to 'see' this inner image with your eyes closed? If so, read the next paragraph, close your eyes, and take yourself visually through that familiar weekly trip.

Way 2 - Visualising the familiar

Let's go to the supermarket. Most of us do that on a regular basis. Imagine the scenario in more detail. Like remembering you need to get a special ingredient for a meal from the supermarket, and then getting a 'flash image' of its location – where exactly you last saw it. (This may help to explain the huge frustration some customers feel when the item they want has been relocated by the sales staff!)

Way 3 - Your personal image/concept balance

In a society where 80% of people have a Left Brain bias, it's personally informative to discover the image/concept balance in your own mind.

Remember to alert the 'observer in your mind' before you start.

Persevere. This is important preparation for later writing, the ability to 'go that bit further' & 'do it in new ways'.

The Learning Journal

You will need a plain paper journal so you can record both words and pictures. That is, your research into greater awareness of how you personally process images and the images themselves. This journal will serve you in four ways.

*   Provide a record of your personal learning journey into images. So you fully appreciate the substantial creative benefits of doing imagework.

*   Record your changing appreciations. This is subtle but it's also the place of personal insights. It'll take you places no teacher can do.

*   A huge difference exists between thinking you know something (it's in your head at the moment) and recording it so you can reflect further – perhaps much later – on its value. By writing it down, you *concretise* it, which pleases the Right Brain method of functioning.

*   Journaling or diarising is part of being a writer. It's a natural way of getting into freeflow state, so the movement from thought or image to its recording becomes easy.

Way 4 – The dynamic interactive approach to inner images

For a week, whenever you have a problem to solve or a task to deal with – especially if it requires you to be pro-active – become aware of whether answers come as words or images. i.e. Whether it arises first from your Left Brain, or from your Right Brain. This is a dynamic way because it requires you develop personal awareness of your brain function. It's interactive because you are putting yourself into a feedback loop – as observer in your own mind.

Way 5 – Taking control of your image/concept balance

After you have researched your own brain functioning, put a percentage on your natural as-of-now image-to-concept reliance and record it in your journal.

As you become more aware (through the services of the 'observer in your mind') whether you favour concepts or images, start to take control. Increase your image-reliance, deliberately seek an image to enhance the concept.

The ideal balance which, hopefully you will attain with a little practice, is one where it's equally easy to reach for an image AND a concept in response to the daily round of decision making and activity.

Creativity – students' perspectives

Right Brain learning

One of the most important things I learned, as a teacher, is the value of *getting students' ideas first*. Then I add my own to fill out the picture. To me, this is an easy and natural way to expand a knowledge-base. It draws on the perceptions of the whole group, rather than prioritises teacher's views. It's *sourced* with the *learners*.

Giving power to students breaks down many barriers. They feel encouraged to speak and immediately start interacting as a group which has the effect of empowering them in later writing tasks. 'Being heard' cannot be overestimated. It banishes fear and raises confidence.

To pretend these issues aren't central to how a writing class functions is a mistake.

Good speakers on writing amuse, entertain and sometimes enlighten and educate us a little through anecdotes. But nothing beats doing and sharing it.

I once asked a new mixed group of students – lawyers, professional women, a housebound young mum – not to *define* creativity (the dictionary does that!) but to work up a list of what they associated with that word. What creativity means to them in its broadest sense.

Students' understanding of creativity

1   Imagination
2   Expressing yourself
3   Ability to touch other people
4   Originality
5   Jobs it'd adhere to.
6   Artistic
7   Release

8   Making something new
9   Painting pictures with words
10   Increasing self-esteem, the more creative you are
11   Me-time
12   Self-belief
13   Spontaneity
14   Improves memory
15   Increasing knowledge (research)
16   Filling a void
17   Insight – into the subject + personal motivations and those of others
18   Increasing self-knowledge
19   Making own rules
20   Natural but tends to be suppressed
21   Widening horizons
22   Improving flexibility of own thinking
23   Helps problem solving
24   Fun

My learning from students' understanding of creativity

A good way to relate to or engage with ('engage with' is a writerly expression) a piece of writing if you want to learn from it and develop its inherent potential is to ask yourself these questions.

1 What surprised me? i.e. What wasn't I expecting?
2 What did I learn?
3 What's my new understanding?

As an example of how this works, I asked myself these three questions of the Student List of their definition of Creativity. There were three surprises.

1 The surprises

- The students' focus on the effects of creativity.
  The perceived personal benefits to being creative and how it touched other areas of their lives.
- The students' awareness of the cultural attitude towards creativity generally.

- The fact none of them mentioned the physical source of human creativity – the Right Brain and its image-speak.

2 What I learned

From this, I learned the students identified a mismatch between a personal and a cultural view of creativity. They had discovered the secret for themselves, but were aware of a very different public image of creativity's status.

3 My new understanding

This concerned the work we were about to do. For greater Right Brain reliance would naturally strengthen students' innate creativity. The fact no-one flagged up Right Brain on this broad I.D. of Creativity List gave me pause, and still does.

This exercise left me with just one question.

How long will it take for the knowledge that creativity is Right Brain sourced to become part of the understanding of all writers who want to be, in any way, 'creative'?

Writer Tip - Reflection as a Writer Skill

Reflection, thinking about how we relate to information presented to us, is a back-up writer skill. How information fits our current perceptions, whether it tweaks, enlarges, radically changes, empowers or turns upside down our current understanding. What effect does this new information have on us so that we isolate what is personally useful? If it gets passed over with the 'oh, that's interesting' reaction, we cut off too soon. Brain-friendly learning sources state we learn only 10% of what we read, compared to 80% of what we personally experience.

Personalised I.D. of Creativity & the Learning Journal

Effective research is a learnt skill, involving reviewing a lot of data to sort out what's important and relevant for a current project.

The research to ascertain your I.D. of Creativity as of now requires you look inside yourself rather than outside for answers. If your response is 'I don't know what I think/feel/believe', this indicates you need to spend time with yourself, quietly developing this inner knowing.

Writer Tip
Saying things in a specific rather than a general way reveals fine distinctions that lead to new understandings. It also sharpens your writing and is personally validating – the opposite experience to ticking boxes.

The 24 points that sum up a group of students' understanding of creativity opens up this subject. It allows you to view a new writing group's perceptions of creativity and respond to that list in a way that is meaningful to you.

In your Learning Journal record:
what creativity means to you as of now.
This may involve some of the 24 points mentioned, or spark ideas not included on that list but which to you are important. Or you may like to rephrase one or two of them.

The issue is you engage with what creativity means to you. This is your startpoint and you can refer back to it later on to see what's altered or grown. You will then have a record of that learning journey. It will be more than just a record for it will give you insights into how you personally learn, what works well for you, and what changes you'd make if doing something like it again. This brings a level of awareness to what you are doing which is not normally present in learning situations. Simultaneously it contributes to the ability to become 'an observer in your mind' and this is a back-up writer skill.

Starmark what you'd like to personally increase or want more of generally in terms of creativity. By turning this into a personal experience, you move from the 10% to 80% learning position. So make it meaningful; an active rather than a passive experience.

More research with students

One reason I chose to do my research through diarising with my students was because I strongly sensed a mismatch between my goals for them, and their goals for themselves.

Initially I assumed all people attending Creative writing classes did so because they wanted to be published, and probably as quickly as possible. Indeed, this was true for some. But my research revealed 21 reasons other than 'I want to be published' that explain why students enrol for classes. The reasons they gave were:

Because I:
1   love writing.
2   want to make money.

3	want to write a best-seller.
4	have a fantasy about being a second Barbara Cartland, Sue Townsend, Jeffrey Archer...
5	want to share my experiences.
6	have to write.
7	want social contact.
8	love listening to other people's work.
9	meet like-minded people.
10	want criticism.
11	want to learn.
12	enjoy it.
13	relax when writing.
14	have to get out of the house to take part.
15	get ideas.
16	get direction.
17	love the homeworks!
18	like being told what to do.
19	meet nice people.
20	stop writing if I don't come to classes.
21	am more motivated in term-time.

Outer reliance/inner reliance balance

The balance between outer and inner reliance within this list is interesting in itself. This book is about developing that inner reliance which is the source of personal creativity so that negative reasons melt away!

Word-association game - a creative approach

A creative way to engage ('engage' is a writerly term meaning 'become involved with') regarding the students' list is to play the word association game. Word association games are often used as warm-ups in creative writing sessions, because they reveal subjective associations. Subjectivity is integral to the writer experience – essential to developing what is called, in literary circles, the 'Writer's Voice' and is a Right Brain quality.

Once you have chosen your personal favourites from the list, find ten words or phrases you associate with that reason. Then, if you can, top the ten off with an image which 'describes it visually for you'.

There's no right or wrong with creative exercises. It's all about subjectivity – finding what is meaningful to you and exploring a personal associative network.

- *Expressing yourself* - Ease, lack of formality, being completely oneself, breaking social taboos, enjoying others' doing so, freed up. *Image...* a raucous teenage party with a lot of shrieking.
- *Helps problem solving...* Relief, removal of worry, can move forward, before laughter. *Image...* a person haking their head and laughing at the same time.
- *Self-belief...* Anger at personal wimpishness, 'how could I have believed that?', a reinvented personality. *Image...* a snow-capped mountain.
- *Widening horizons...* Extension, freedom, see more, understand more. Privileged. *Image...* the sea.
- *Painting pictures with words...* an achievement indeed!, detail, zen-like, simple, startling. *Image...* the artist at his easel.
- *Spontaneity...* The current belief we create our own reality, total surprise. *Image...* children at play.
- *Increasing self-esteem, the more creative you are...* joy of invention, finding things within *Image...* Person, arms outstretched, thumping the air in successive gestures of 'Yes'!
- *Natural but tends to be suppressed...* What will friends think?, fear of disapproval. *Image...* the lone writer -with or without garret.
- *Improves flexibility of thinking...* no more 'same old', a new mind, using the mind differently, *Image...* A young tree bending – but not breaking – in a strong wind.
- *Imagination...* Freedom of thought, not constrained by reality, unhindered by practicality. *Image...* a shooting star.
- *Ability to touch other people...* Empathy, moments of sympatico, a heartlink, a mindmeld. *Image...* hands - and paws! - linking across the world.
- *Originality....*New thoughts, fresh associations, bright ideas, real paradigm shifts. *Image...* two Earths in a

binary... one consisting of water, the other of land.

- *Discovery...* Sense of adventure, living my characters' lives, sharing their emotions. *Image...* setting out on a journey with a rucksack and boots.

- *A love of creativity expressed through writing...* Passion, the best motivation of all, *Image...* a starlit night in winter with the aurora borealis putting on a fine display.

This word association game acts as both clearing house for many ideas that are rarely directly expressed, and a way to examine aspects of creativity that are meaningful to you. It may even open up specific directions in terms of development as a writer. The exercise acted as a stepping stone, a way to get to somewhere far more important, relevant – into what is deeply and personally fascinating. This is natural creative growth in action.

Something to visualise
Background on Visualisation

We need to understand visualisation as an underused human skill, as well as a personal power source. Both self-healing and self-development rely extensively on visualisation.

Visualisation is a powerful personal tool with great credibility - a real 'free gift' to writers!

Spend ten minutes a day practising visualising. Five minutes to do the visualisation, and five minutes to record your impressions.

See if regular visualisation practice makes a difference generally to your perceptions. Record any differences in your Learning Journal.

Visualising works as an antidote to a Left Brain bias, as a mind refresh, to give yourself a Right Brain boost and to enrich your writing style.

The visualisation - Colour

Whatever comes into your mind, give it brighter primary colours than usual. Make it more colourful than in reality.

To help you stay focused on the spectrum of colour,

invite onto the inner screen of your mind whatever feels most colourful to you.

Watch what colour does when you constantly refocus on it. This should be a relaxing pleasant exercise that simply increases colour awareness. Record the experience.

4 Creativity's identity

'*More has been discovered about how the human brain works in the last 15 years than in all history to date.*'

From a writer's viewpoint, this means we are now in a position to work with the natural functioning of the brain. The logical left brain speaks in words and concepts. The creative Right Brain communicates only through images. This is why it is so important to learn, listen to, and engage with the image-speak of your Right Brain, if you wish to be creative. Especially if you suspect you are one of the 80% of people in western society who are Left Brain dominant.

Multidimensionality & Commonality

A few things need to be established about Right Brain functioning.

    1 Its broad principles apply to us all.

    2 The specific functioning of the Right Brain in any one human being is unique. The easy way to appreciate this is by analogy. No two snowflakes are identical either!

    If you choose to research Right Brain creativity, one of the first things you may notice is the variety of interpretation, set out through that *Left Brain function,* words.

The double filter

It's important to realise we all deal with perceptions that go through two filters. The first filter is the physical set-up of any one particular brain which is slightly and sometimes markedly different to everyone else's. The second filter is the one resulting from *development.* That is, how the individual's brain has been used, influenced, especially in the formative years, through life.

    This double filter is a reinvention of the old-fashioned 'nature-or-nurture' debate. This debate used to centre on which was believed to be *dominant* in human development.

By reframing the nature-or-nurture debate as a double filter on our perceptions, we give it a new and dynamic meaning. In reality, the dominant formative influence, nature or nurture, will depend on the individual concerned.

Golden Guideline

If it comes out of your head, own it. It's meaningful to you. Though it may take you a while to decode its symbology. Don't be in a hurry to categorise any image as negative or positive. By refusing to work with an image you initially dislike, - because of its immediate and superficial associations - you cut off from deeper learning. This is where patience with oneself is important.

Look to the model of J.K Rowling as illustrative. Before the advent of Hogwarts, there were many stories about witch and wizard schools. None of them covered seven years of a young person's life or were so fully realised, drawing off all-time mythology and reinventing it to suit the story. With Harry Potter, J.K. Rowling went further than any previous children's writer into the fantasy school theme and reaped the reward for doing so.

The human dynamic multi-interactive system as evolving image

This concept is really simple. Technologically, for communication, we've moved from telephone exchanges, through computers to the internet and broadband. Our human ability to multitask – even the invention of the concept - points to human evolution in understanding. Alongside the development in the communication-network runs a parallel understanding concerning the brain's capability.

Writer Tip

Creative writers translate or underpin an idea, with a known or at least imaginable physical reality that is large enough to carry the fullness of their original inspiration. That physical reality also has to fulfil a second equally important requirement. It must be a fictional reality that the average reader can and will relate to easily. The original idea may come in the form of an intuitive feeling. It can take years to find a form – not genre, but form – scenario, focus, language, development, characters, that can carry that idea.

This is where the image excels because it draws on unconscious knowing. That is, knowing we possess in image-form in our Right Brains but are not consciously aware through normal Left Brain perceptions.

Left Brain logical, Right Brain AR-tistic

The Left Brain logical, Right Brain artistic tag needs flagging up repeatedly. Especially if you have believed all your life in the superiority of the Left Brain

The mnemonic l – logical, ar – artistic, aids memory. The poet in us appreciates the alliterative l – logical, and sound-alike in ar-artistic.

The Right Brain/Left Brain skills

Here's a Right Brain/Left Brain list of attributes.

	RIGHT BRAIN	LEFT BRAIN
1	*Images and symbols*	*Language and words*
2	Creative	Mathematical
3	Visual	Verbal
4	Concrete	Abstract
5	*wholistic**	Conceptual
6	Intuitive	Intellectual
7	Random	Logical
8	Synthesising	Critical
9	Relational	Analytical
10	Divergent	Convergent
11	Non-linear	Linear
12	Simultaneous	Successive
13	Infinitive	Sequential
14	Imagination rules	Facts rule
15	Big picture oriented	Detail oriented
16	Looks at wholes	Looks at parts
17	Colour	Black and white
18	Subjective	Objective
19	Risk-taking	Safe
20	Sense-based	Rational

Remember

* *wholistic** is deliberately spelt with a 'w' to reinforce its connections with things seen in the round, as wholes. This spelling dissociates the meaning of the word normally spelt holistic from holes, holey and things holy.

Some of these pairs are not absolute opposites. Neither are these two lists an exhaustive presentation of human brain skills. They are selected specifically to demonstrate what becomes available to you as a writer, from your Right Brain, once you choose to engage with images rather than just words.

Right Brain language of image-speak

Writer Tip
New writers are encouraged to think in terms of anecdotes – little stories which give readers pictures – to lighten the text and make the reading more enjoyable.

As soon as we use words, we automatically put ourselves in Left Brain mode. Developing the Right Brain gives whole pictures. From a whole picture, the intricacy of the relationships between all its parts emerges, rather like happens when understanding how an ecosystem works. Imagework makes these connections and exactly how they interact visible, so they stand out. This brings these interconnections to your attention.

You may wonder what image underpins this book. The answer is 'a tight weave'. (See Chapter 16).

A cross-over image to help reorientate

Here's a useful dynamic image to take you through any remaining resistance to using imagery. It's like having to drive on the other side of the road, the opposite to what you are used to doing. It carries a little initial anxiety, wobbliness, but once you are on another continent and on holiday and have been driving on the opposite side of the road for just a short time, a new sense of power and freedom takes over, replaces and overturns doubts. The feeling and feeding of adventure and discovery lead the way.

Learning to speak both languages of the human brain with equal facility – a readiness to call up image or concept – is both a writer-skill and a way to rebalance the brain.

Defining a Brainview (as in 'worldview')

By brainview I mean the way we look at our own minds and their functioning. The choices of ways to define a brainview are immense, once we move into the personalised, pro-active and interactive domain. Remember though, throughout, to prioritise images over concepts.

Criticism v. creativity

To present criticism as an opposite of creativity is not new. Modern books on writing of the 'freeing-up the-writer-within' type often spend several chapters on the subject of the 'inner critic'. They go into great detail (a Left Brain skill) concerning what writers can and must do to control the inner critic, depower it and generally redefine its role in writing contexts so it works for you rather than against you.

Such is the power of the Left Brain to dominate.

The cultural filter of literary criticism

One of my first jobs, as a writing teacher, is to undo the tangle produced by confusing 'literary criticism' or any sort of 'criticism' with what a writing class is about. Primarily, a writing class is about encouraging and developing creativity.

The personal filter of criticism

Pause for a moment and feel how deeply criticism is grooved into our psyches. Though you may have to go to a real event in your life to contact the feeling, try then to forget *the event* and just focus on re-experiencing the *feelings*.

Criticism lives within our experience as learners and is activated by finding ourselves 'a student' again. To this potent and automatic connection between learning and not-getting-it-right-first-time add just a smidgen of under confidence.

It shocked me that, when it comes to sharing their writing, professional people can be quite as sensitive as those with no qualifications. The esteem they naturally possess in their work-a-day world does not carry over. Very often a piece of writing is introduced to a group by saying, in one form or another, how bad it is. Generally, professional people have acquired a level of education that makes writing a basic skill and this level of under confidence is therefore quite inappropriate. Of course teachers find ways to encourage and support their development as writers.

Writer Tip
To write with power, we need to develop the capability of writing from our strongest emotions. To begin this process, fiction writers call up the emotion-attached-to-a-personal-life-event and then transfer the fullness of the emotion to the fictional characters in the situation they are writing about.

Writer Tip
The double filter is a wonderful fictional device to prevent your reader from accessing the truth until the end of a story. The twist ending story or the double-twist is the right place for a writer to use the double filter. But it takes a little effort to shift it to this context where it serves rather than rules the writer.

Transforming the double filter

The double filter is far more powerful than a single filter, it is a stopper on the truth emerging. You must want to get beneath surface-appearances as well as become an 'observer in your own mind'. This is a simple idea, simpler than multi-tasking. Our fantastic brains are quite capable of holding twin foci at the same time and assigning one focus to being an observer of our own actions as we do them.

Something to visualise
The visualisation - Colour bonanza

Can you remember times in your life when your awareness of colour was particularly strong? A childhood holiday time perhaps, or a visit to another culture?

When you have located several, close your eyes and, in imagination, move between them. As much as you can, fully experience the colour sensations of each experience. Now see if you can locate any other commonality, things that are similar or the same about them. High levels of anticipation, great enjoyment, or a sense of adventure emotionally heighten experiences. The mood and feelings, that accompanying these colour-rich experiences are important sources to reconnect to when writing.

Ways into Image: Start a personal brainview

Way 1 Prioritise the Right Brain list.

Record this in your journal

In your Learning Journal, highlight or re-order the 20 attributes from the Right Brain skills list to suit your taste and current needs as a writer. Bring to the top of the list those Right Brain skills you know will be particularly useful to you, and enrich your writing, or ones you instinctively feel will make the writing process easier. It's interacting with the Right Brain list that's important at this stage.

You might want to expand on a few of the points. Begin sentences with 'It intrigues me...' or 'It surprised me...' Remember, the personal reaction is the one most meaningful to you and most important in overall learning.

Remember you cannot prioritise images or drawing,

any more than you can prioritise words. Image-speak is the Right Brain language. In the same way as words constitute the Left Brain language.

Way 2 – Personalise the Right Brain list.

As a writer you need to use/develop perseverance, stamina and a love, curiosity or fascination that drives a desire to go deeper into process of writing and creativity.

Write down the benefits - as you perceive them now – offered by this Right Brain skill. Access and claim its long term value to your development as a writer. Later, do a reality-check on perceived and actual benefits - it will form a deep source of personal learning. The surprises are mind-changing and root you into a deeper level of learning and deeper creativity.

It's trite but true that the more you put in, the more you get out.

5 Understanding & mastering Right Brain I.D.

This chapter offers:

- Overviews on Right Brain I.D.
- Clustering as a Left Brain overview of Right Brain I.D.
- A whole brain appreciation of brain functioning
- A new personalised brainview

Overview on purpose and function of this chapter

This chapter is about a brain-based approach to both commonality and the uniqueness of the creative experience. That is, an understanding filtered through how our brains work - the commonality - and how our individual brains work - the uniqueness.

Both Left Brain and Right Brain ways to define and encapsulate overviews concerning Right Brain I.D. are worthwhile because they supply self knowledge about how our brains currently operate. That is, the need to recognise the likelihood of Left Brain bias while encouraging a more Right Brain appreciation.

With that remit in mind, this chapter explores one Left Brain way of approaching a mega overview - clustering or chunking. By showing how clustering works we attain a Left Brain based appreciation of Right Brain skills.

While writing this chapter, the overview at the image-level changed for me. It literally evolved as I was writing the chapter. The first image was of seven overlapping different coloured discs with a yellow central disc representing the visual cluster which united them all.

The *evolved* image is of a six-petalled flower with the flower's heart symbolising image-speak.

7 overlapping discs

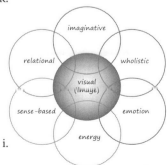

See colour illustration on page i.

31

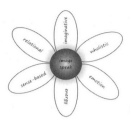

A six - petalled flower

See colour illustration on page ii.

The ultimate test for 'what works for you' is how memorable it is. The goal of all learning is it be remembered and applied. So, the invitation to you here, and again at the end of this chapter is to find for yourself an image - a personal one - that encapsulates your present understanding of your Right Brain I.D. You may have a similar experience to mine - and find a better more memorable image as you proceed.

This is not about a *choice* between Right Brain and Left Brain overviews. That's too simplistic and misses the point. By starting with an image which is then decoded by the Left Brain, we key into our natural human brain-based way to learn and start to move towards the real goal - whole brain learning.

By missing out the Right Brain input at the overview level, I believe we make learning harder for ourselves because we are working with half the brain's natural functioning. We certainly make our understanding more intellectual and Left Brain. Consequently, it's less creative because the Right Brain is factored out.

Clearly, the choice between *sourcing* overviews Right Brain or Left Brain has implications for all learning, not just learning about creativity and Right Brain I.D. The bonus here is you have an opportunity to test using images as overviews - the Right Brain approach - as against a technique like clustering - a Left Brain approach. Find out which one works best. Which one you *remember*.

This chapter is another way to monitor a personal Left Brain bias. As you read this chapter monitor your response to clustering as a personal learning technique. We all have different learning styles but we do need to factor in the Left Brain bias of clustering at the start. Without that awareness, we may not realise this little test offers a great opportunity to balance our learning styles at a brain-based level.

First impressions of Right Brain I.D.

For anyone, the quantum nature of Right Brain functioning – signalled by 'simultaneous' being one of its attributes – may come as a surprise.

Clusters are a recognised memory aid. For the writer, clustering shows how and where a group of Right Brain functions serve a writer's needs. There is overlap within the seven clusters, but the overlap itself acts to link them together – like seven overlapping spheres. Obviously, this diagrammatic representation is a much simplified way of looking at Right Brain functioning. For the writer, it makes clear the links which then form the source of many writer skills.

The Seven Clusters

The seven clusters are:
Emotion
Visual
*Wholistic**
Relational
Imaginative
Sense-based
Energy

Initially you may wonder why such depth in understanding is necessary for a writer. It's necessary because these links are not in place in our minds. If we've had a conventional education, we certainly haven't been taught to use the creative side of our minds with the same facility as the logical side and therefore have to undertake the job of reprogramming ourselves. Through using the technique of clustering or chunking, we highlight the direct links between Right Brain source and writer skill.

It isn't so much that it's important to know where exactly it's coming from in our heads. Though that does fascinate some writers! It's more to do with a sense of control, a greater awareness of the full nature of the amazing human brain.

For instance, there can be a huge mismatch between 'how we feel' (subjective evaluation) and 'how it is'. If we act too much from negative feelings we may block ourselves and cut off from all the potential ready, waiting and available in our Right Brains. Our inner world shrinks when it should be expanding and growing.

Confidence is, and remains, a major issue for many students of writing. When people have a deep appreciation of Right Brain functioning, with it comes a sense of control and mastery. This deeper understanding is not so easily eroded by careless superficial comments or cultural perceptions.

This fuller understanding of how our brains work gives you the chance to check out and test the general principles and begin the fine distinctions which will lead to more control and mastery of your own creativity and writing.

This leads us to an important point. If making the 'fine distinctions' happens at too early a stage, when you are still in the dark about how to get the best out of your Right Brain, it can result in muddled thinking.

Straightaway, we can identify three muddles that arise from restricted thinking. That is, cutting off too soon without factoring in the great commonalities in human brain function.

1, The claim of individuality

To say 'my brain works differently to everyone else's' is absolutely true but we all, particularly writers, need to maximise on our skills base. That begins by understanding the great commonalities in human brain function.

2, Fear, version 1 – fear of the subconscious

There used to be, and still is, a fear in some people concerning their subconscious, what they might find there. Things brought into the light – of consciousness – tend to look less terrifying than 'the unknown'. (Apparently the greatest human fear is 'Fear of the Unknown'.) Antediluvian this belief may appear, but it is still around. This belief clashes with any instruction or advice to 'explore the inner world' – as you would a new place you visited - with a sense of discovery, anticipation and heightened awareness.

3, Fear, version 2 – fear of loss of magic

There is an opposite reason to not explore your own

mind 'too much'. Again, it is fear based. The muddle here concerns a fear of losing the magic by 'knowing too much'. The belief is that, by having a full understanding of brain functioning, its magical qualities may be lost to us in the process. In fact, the opposite happens. The *real* magic – the quantum quality – surfaces and comes through into our writing.

The twisted reasoning concerning the loss of magic by knowing too much borrows off an old childhood-to-adulthood perception, another negative belief that the more we know, the less magical and miraculous the world appears. It's a plea to value innocence, but it muddles ignorance with innocence and so is unhelpful.

These three muddles - a perceived attack on individuality backed by two fears - can lead to a treble block. Any one of these three muddles, though not necessarily talked about, nevertheless influence *attitude*. If not talked about, their effect is often more powerful, because it works subconsciously. Its hidden quality makes it more effective in stopping people from wholeheartedly exploring and embracing their own creativity.

These are emotional reactions. We need to take a close look at emotion. First, because it is not, directly, a Right Brain function. Nevertheless, its influence on the Right Brain is enormous. We detect emotion's presence through locating subjectivity, sense-based writing, and the relational in the Right Brain.

The place of emotion

A brain-based appreciation of emotion requires us to take a different view of the brain. Not a Right Brain/Left Brain one – the horizontal look, but a vertical take. The vertical perspective reveals the triune brain, in three parts, each part wrapped over the one beneath it. At the base is the old reptilian brain, responsible for the survival instinct. On top of that is the limbic system or emotional brain and on top of that is the cortex in charge of mental functioning.

One distinction between Right and Left Brain functioning is the Right Brain attribute of subjectivity and the Left Brain one's of *objectivity*. Left Brain objective ties in with logical, analytical, deductive reasoning.

Right Brain *subjective* links with the individual personal associations accessed through Right Brain work – the 'felt response' and emotional intelligence naturally draw on emotion. Experientially, we know the immediate emotional response we have to a picture which strikes us as either beautiful or terrifying. The link between the Right Brain and the limbic system of emotion is strong. Nevertheless it is the limbic system itself which is responsible for emotion, and this includes five distinct functions.

Emotional responses
Control of emotions
Mood
Motivation
Pain and pleasure sensations

Writer Tip

To take a brain-based view of ourselves – the system reflecting on itself – is a dissociative move, zen-like. This helps both when learning to see in overviews and becoming 'an observer in your own mind'. It puts you on the path to the 'Inner Game' approach to learning where increased self-awareness is key to progress.

Emotion as a whole body experience

Candace Pert, author of *Molecules of Emotion* (Simon & Shuster 0671033972) was the first neuroscientist to prove that every cell in the human body has an emotional connector. This was a big scientific breakthrough and its ramifications are enormous, particularly, of course, in the medical field. But it alters the view that emotion is confined to the limbic system and the popular approach of reading body language. That is, the body 'does things' of which the owner may not be aware which gives away feelings. Like the eye's pupil dilation, red-faced anger, the kicking foot, the fig-leaf hand-pose of the under confident speaker, the relaxed arms-folded laid-back body posture or the intense forward position adopted by people at meetings.

Pert's research verifies emotion's whole body status at cell level. As positive thinking is an emotion-based choice, its influence too registers throughout the whole human body. Simply by realising that any emotion 'you' feel is felt by all your millions of body cells may help to explain why the balanced viewpoint – neither wholly analytical nor over-emotional – is sometimes difficult to attain. This is particularly so in our age of spin when objective, far-sighted and long-term good are not everyone's goals.

The effect of writing on the writer

When people first start writing 'letting it all hang out' – that student association with creativity – it can be an enormously liberating experience simply because the veto on expressing emotion is removed. Or it may have the opposite effect – certain new writers feel threatened by the 'exposure' writing demands of feelings. One older student of mine who loved writing stated *'I could never be a proper writer. It requires too much self-exposure.'* I don't think he is right because we can choose what sort of writing we do and this is part of the process of discovery, particularly if we are not initially drawn to one particular genre.

This is an echo of the childhood question... what do I want to do or be when I grow up? Some youngsters know exactly what they want to do; others have an inkling of a direction based on their strengths, possibly, but no specific career in mind.

'Keep searching' can strike as bleak advice. To read omnivorously opens the mind to the possible. But it needs the other sort of research too... research into our own creative minds if we are not to end up as hack writers, just doing it as a job, instead of writing from the heart.

Natural Break

Write, for ten minutes, in your Learning Journal, on your relationship with your creative brain. For help, ask your inner child for input. The one who likes to play, imagine and have fun. That frivolous exterior is the invitation to a 'no-holds-barred' mindset. It certainly doesn't mean lack of serious intent. Are there any fear-blocks you need to tackle now?

The seven clusters or six petalled flower image bring together the three earlier lists – key writer skills, student perceptions of creativity, and the Right Brain attributes compiled from various internet sources. Also added are certain Right Brain activities identified as increasing Right Brain activity, such as Brain Gym and role play.

Important fine distinction concerning the clusters

The short paragraph of explanation after each of these clusters begins with how it feeds the *writer* and moves on to how it feeds the *writing*. In the sense used here, the word 'feed' means not just improve, but make easier, grow, facilitate, expand, make more aware as well as learn through doing.

How the seven clusters work for writers
Emotion

This cluster includes:

- Emotion
- Subjective
- Letting it all hang out
- Fun
- Spontaneous

- Intuitive
- Expressing yourself
- Release
- Childlike
- Natural, but tends to be suppressed

At the start, it's the passion and discovering what drives it that the new writer explores. In the development of a writer, there is an initial freedom found in creativity. Later, that sense of creative freedom evolves into exploring specialist areas and interests where those emotions find expression time and again.

Fiction writers express the emotions of their characters, of all those sub-personalities waiting inside to be discovered. Non-fiction writers express their emotions - attached to their beliefs – related to the subject-matter they are writing about.

Visual

This cluster includes:

- Visualisation
- Concrete
- Symbols
- Artistic

- Metaphor
- Images
- Painting pictures with words

The visual, in many and various forms, will be the start point for the rest of this book. It will lead into all Creative writing related areas which is why it's central in the diagram and forms the heart of the six-petalled flower.

Wholistic*

This cluster includes:

- Big picture oriented
- Synthesis
- Looks at wholes
- Infinitive

New writers are often excited by an idea but developing it they find difficult. This is the area where learning to read an image for meaningful detail offers an alternative – and often easier – way of development than 'thinking about an idea'.

Even experienced writers claim that the synopsis is the most difficult piece of writing they have to do. As overviews (looking at wholes) is a Right Brain skill, it's likely the logical left brain is taking over without the writer even realising it. Proof of this happening is when a synopsis begins to look like a précis – a set of linked events devoid of emotion.

Relational

This cluster includes:

- Ability to touch other people
- Increasing self-esteem, the more creative you are
- Self-belief
- Dialoguing
- Me-time
- Role-play

Role-play is highlighted because it increases Right Brain activity. Characters – creating them (some writers say 'giving birth to them') is the major skill offered by the relational cluster where role-playing invented characters is a prime skill. Role play is explored in Chapter 13.

Imaginative

This cluster includes:

- Imagination
- Blue sky thinking
- Risk-taking
- Brainstorming

- *Originality*
- *Divergent thinking*
- *Widening horizons*
- *Improve flexibility of thinking*
- *Making something new*
- *Randomness*
- *Helps problem-solving*

The first thing you notice about this cluster is there's more words here, more links to consider to creative writing. This cluster claims the creative hotline – Imagination itself - but the expansive and new within its remit show this is a fertile and growing place to be and not just a land of daydreams.

Sense-based

This cluster includes:

- *Touch*
- *Sound – including music*
- *Feelings*
- *Taste*
- *Smell*
- *Sight*

This area is familiar ground to all writers, because it is central to the creative writing lexicon. It is part of the working base of creative writing classes. Sense-based writing's ease of explanation and the simplicity of exercises arising from it often make it the first thing to be taught, to emphasise and demonstrate the familiar advice of 'show, don't tell'.

Energy

This cluster includes:

- *Passion*
- *Motivation*
- *Action*
- *Gut-reactions*
- *Spontaneity*
- *Movement – Brain gym*

This seventh cluster may come as a surprise, because it's not usually emphasised. I believe energy is the glue that holds everything together. Without passion you'll never go the distance. Passion is long-term, emotion is of the moment. *Gut reactions* are clear signs you listen to inner knowing. *Motivation* will take you through the rough patches and is superior to discipline. *Spontaneity* keeps you in touch with your inner child. These four – *passion, gut reactions, motivation and spon-*

taneity - originate in the Right Brain and drive a writer's work. Because physical movement is Right Brain too, Brain Gym is today recommended as a quick way to enliven a sluggish mind.

In fictional terms, *action* translates into plot, into deeply knowing that 'what happens next' is the reader's question from the first to the last moment of your story.

Second Natural Break

From looking at each cluster, are there any elements you'd cluster under another head? E.g. I've seen 'Intuition' flagged up as a defining overview to include metaphors, feelings, symbols and body messages. The key point with Right Brain functioning is that it is simultaneous and unique to every individual. Therefore imposing a hierarchical structure of any sort only takes us so far. Also, this book has a definite and deliberate writer-bias, designed to deepen the connection between the wealth of Right Brain functions and ten basic writing skills.

'Infinitive', perhaps, you'd prefer in the Imagination cluster, because you feel its expansiveness has more in common with the fired-up imagination than it does with the mega overview of 'wholistic'*? This is where your personal 'fine distinctions' come into play. In your Learning Journal, move any elements you feel intuitively fit better to a different cluster.

Remember, it is in engaging with what is presented that we both make it our own and start to take it in directions personally satisfying, interesting and exciting.

Diversity of personal responses

In a group situation, a variety of personal responses are expressed on discovering the I.D. of creativity and the centrality of imagework. E.g.:

'*This is how it is supposed to be. I always had a sneaking feeling it was something like this.*' (smugness at being right).

'*This aligns exactly with my experience but no-one ever talks about it!*' (indignation).

'*Why wasn't I told about this at school?*' (anger).

'*It's very interesting but I'm used to my own working methods.*' (reticence to try the new).

'I feel like I'm on the brink of amazing creative discoveries!' (intuiting the truth)!

As we go deeper into understanding the creative human mind, three things stand out.

1   Of all the so-called artistic pursuits, writing is the only Left Brain one. The product – novel, poem, story - is delivered to the public in Left Brain form.

2   Now we have a brain-based view of Right Brain creativity and capability which experts call 'quantum', we need to go beyond incorporating it and integrating it into how we view our minds. We need an entirely new brainview. This new brainview will reflect more accurately our inner creative potential. Without it, we may go on much as before.

3   The term 'paradigm shift' is used to describe a shift to a new level of thinking and awareness. It happens where the effect of the new knowledge is to radically change and overtake earlier limited understanding. The new paradigm helps people see the restrictions or limitations of the old way of doing something, whether less effective, less efficient, underusing natural potential, or holding a mental construct which reflects a limited appreciation of what is actually available.

Consideration of these three facts points us towards and helps us to formulate a new working strategy which involves the Right Brain at every point in the creative process, bar the writing itself.

Image-speak - a new working strategy

A new working strategy starts by practising speaking Right Brain language – familiarising ourselves with the many available forms of image-speak. So any off-putting unfamiliarity is quickly dealt with and put behind us.

This strategy involves a change in working methods. To habitually prefer and source creative projects in Right Brain mode.

This same strategy goes through the whole creative process by favouring working methods that are Right Brain in orientation. Role play, Right Brain-type questioning and interrogation to forward development. (Left Brain questions tend to be closed, shutting down options. Right Brain questions tend to expand and open up a subject.)

It concludes by using Right Brain mode for final synthesis, a way of checking for fullness of development, rounded appreciations and depth of understanding.

This prioritising of the Right Brain at every stage of development is a strategy which requires in the writer, more than anything else, a new awareness of brain use.

Something to visualise
Background on visualisation

A restricted thinking-palate confines the mind to what's in-your-face, as of now. Loosening the boundaries through a range of simple visualisation exercises expands the inner field; provides a wider range to draw on and play on as creative source.

Memory is culturally connected to nostalgia, but that's only one way to frame it.

Children have memories. Older people just have more of them! Sometimes a memory can replay itself in our minds too often or too much. The following exercise is an opportunity to loosen its hold, and play with reality. This exercise also serves as an early move into fictionalising.

As with the colour visualisation in the last chapter, read through the following short section and then try the exercise for yourself.

The visualisation - Memory

The Memory visualisation is in three stages.

1   Visualise a personal memory. Recreate its detail in your mind. Experience it as fully as possible.

2   Now add in - superimpose - the heightened colour you learned to use in the first visualisation. See if you can achieve that same brilliance, depth of colour, in your imagination.

3   Change one thing, just one thing, about this memory. It may be a fundamental or subtle change. E.g. Make yourself older or younger than you were or introduce another person - character. You choose. Record what happened in your Learning Journal.

In your Learning Journal also record:

1   Any remaining resistance to imagework. Be honest. No-one will see it but you. Express it in terms that draw on the felt-sense level, rather than an intellectual appreciation. Apprehension, doubts, 'is this worthwhile?' are legitimate feelings, especially if you have never done anything like this before. Try to sense if there is any movement, a softening in attitude. Have you learned anything so far which encourages the opposite reaction – can't wait to try it!?

2   Which cluster of the Right Brain skills most attracts you? Which cluster do you feel you already know and is easily accessible to you now, and which cluster contains the 'must-haves'?

3   List the writer skills you'd like to uprate and note what Right Brain quality is back of them.

The Personalised Brainview

To continue to hold the old paradigm of a Left Brain dominant model, i.e. *Left Brain knows best,* will weaken or even completely sabotage creativity. To invent for ourselves a new, original self-designed brainview which values imagery as a personal goldmine will help enormously in the stakes of giving the Right Brain the credibility it deserves.

Invite an image that gives you a new brainview. One that satisfies you personally, incorporates or reflects the learning important to you and is memorable. Then draw it. Make notes in your Learning Journal about its qualities. The more you personalise it, give it specific characteristics, the more memorable it will be to you.

6   Relating to
Right Brain I.D.

Learning personal image-speak

Unless you are artistic, imagery quickly acquires the status of being a lesser function of the modern intelligent human being. Recall one of the questions raised in Chapter 1.

'How come it has taken until the 21st century for im-agework to be accepted as a key source for writers?'

Cultural perceptions, Left Brain bias, habitual thinking styles and categorisations that work against *joined-up thinking* all play a part.

First we need to develop a personal relationship with our own inner imagery over time. On top of which we have to learn to read and interpret our own symbology.

Reframing image-speak

As the move away from our normal communication style – words – increases through use of terms like 'simultaneous, *wholistic**, synthesising, random, divergent and intuitive', unless we have a deep trust in a personal sense of 'inner knowing' we may feel, psychologically, on quicksand. This is highly relevant in a culture where 'inner knowing' is not fostered and hallmarked as a great personal trait. The culture's learning focus is on the acquisition of outer skills for career; not inner skills for lifelong growth. This includes many sorts of growth – growth of ideas for writing, for creativity and story-weaving, as well as personal growth. These are all roles where image-speak excels. What's more, the Right Brain doesn't distinguish between them. It doesn't categorise them into different types of growth. That's Left Brain. So at any one time, an image may reveal things to you that you were not expecting. This is the *'leaky margin effect'* which causes another sort of confusion. If a writer doesn't instantly 'get the meaning' from a drawing, or actively dislikes a self-generated image, that may be enough to discourage further exploration. It also explains why a first reaction to a self-generated image may be 'it's impenetrable'. This happens because the focus is too narrow. You haven't yet found the overview (Right Brain) where the meanings of your drawing will leap out at you. Of course, this also explains why writers may not travel very far down this road. In the context of learning a new language, it's like going no further than being able to say 'yes', 'no', and 'how much is it?'

The Virtuous Circle in relation to imagery for writers

The Virtuous circle is less well-known than the vicious one. As writers develop, particularly those who wish to engage the more creative forms - novelists, poets, fiction-writers and playwrights – this inner reliance and the necessity for it increases. So a learning loop is set up. Imagework deepens understanding in *wholistic** ways; the subjective, visual and concrete translate it into fictional scenarios in the mind, and the writer learns to deeply trust and believe in a personal inner process. They feed each other and the growth is, of course, simultaneous, as in organic. It happens all at the same time, and this is where and why the writer experiences enormous personal satisfaction in doing it. 'Getting lost in writing' becomes as easy as 'getting lost in music'. The whole brain is involved in the process. For writers, the translation into words – that final Left Brain move – guarantees whole brain participation.

So now you know, at the brain-based level, what it is that fiction writers and poets alike share.

Sometimes, doing the opposite of the conventional illuminates something normally tagged mysterious or weird. The following is a projected – and more intimate and personalised - trip into the process of imagework for writers. The wobbly bits are presented as hurdles to be negotiated. My intention is to illuminate the doubts and uncertainties that any writer who is a non-artist is bound to experience when doing imagework for the first time. Even if a person is wonderfully enthusiastic, some of these hurdles require real mental leaps. Writing and imagery are inner games in the sense used in sports training. Yet we have an expectation of, and are habituated to rely on outer guidance, so this too biases our feelings and appreciations.

If 'Am I doing this right?' or 'I wish I could show the author of this book this drawing' are running in your mind, it's a sign you need to deepen that inner reliance. The meaning I would take from your drawing or image might ring no bells for you at all. This happens because my symbolic associations or personal associative network are as subjective (Right Brain again) as are yours. And, and, - and this is the important bit – yours are far more valid! To listen or take notice of my 'reading' of your drawing could undermine and take away from developing that vital inner direction you need to learn to trust in yourself.

In Right Brain style, many ways are offered into imagery in this book, and this gives (metaphorically) many 'handles' on process.

Way 1

Understanding Right Brain I.D. begins with using its language – image-speak. Next we need to remind ourselves of what it is exactly we are contacting through using image-speak. All the distinctive Right Brain qualities and functions become available as soon as we start drawing.

From the writer's viewpoint, these Right Brain qualities offer divergent, random, non-linear and imaginative development, a range of overviews reliant on the *wholistic** Right Brain function leading to synthesis, fictional characters (relational) role-played by the writer, to the final sense-based concrete expression through words on paper.

Creative process isn't usually expressed in these terms, where the Right Brain's role is located as source every time. Creative process isn't given this contextualisation, these frameworks to constantly reinforce the need to employ Right Brain strategies. Colloquially, to ensure the Right Brain is 'on board' and we, as wordsmiths, writers, without realising it, haven't slipped into Left Brain mode.

Remember, Left Brain mode is the one favoured by the whole of western culture. When we have an inbuilt bias we are unconscious of, which is the situation 80% of us in western culture face, the relearning process is more complicated than first appears.

First we have to recognise and then to remind ourselves of the bias. This is more difficult because it is a lifelong habit. For the majority of us, Left Brain is our habitual way of doing, thinking and processing. In order to begin to change anything, we have to develop sensitivity for something we previously were not aware of. It requires a degree of mental vigilance to achieve and hold this awareness, to break this lifelong habit. It's not addictive, like drugs, but it's accepted by the culture, a habit since childhood, and unconscious.

Not only do we have to remind ourselves of the bias, we have to do so at appropriate moments. Unfortunately, these are likely to be those when our minds are fully occupied. There's a saying - 'the last thing learned is the first to be forgotten'.

Way 2

Professional writers giving talks to writing groups often say they have a notice pinned up over their computer. In large letters this notice says **'Make a scene of it!'**

Go one step further. Personalise each of the 20 Right Brain skills – and any other words you associate with personal creativity – and pin them up around your workspace. This keeps the diverse range of skills available through image-speak permanently within sight.

Way 3

Learn image-speak as the language of the Right Brain, the heart, personal development and, most important of all for writers, the language of creativity.

Nothing less than this will have much effect on the writer who is a non-artist.

How Left Brain bias sabotages image-speak

The habitual way of organising our thinking is Left Brain dominant. That's a deeply ingrained pattern, a complex of behaviour constructed in our heads over a lifetime. It's also the culture's programming to ensure we fit in and usefully contribute to the (reasonably) smooth running of society. This is the everyday world.

7 hurdles to learning image-speak

This is the secret to learning image-speak.

Hurdle 1

Turn to image, rather than concept, first. Don't think – unless thoughts want to come. Just draw. Just follow a line, a fancy, a whim. Literally, let the drawing lead the way. Colour, shape, thickness of stroke, direction, pattern, size. Let it happen. Draw with the sort of mindset you use for a freewrite – to see where it goes and leads.

Hurdle 2

When you've finished, look at your drawing. And listen to the thoughts that come, with a finger poised, ready, to activate the mental 'delete' button on anything negative or judgemental about its artistic merit that comes to mind. Reframe all negative comments concerning the imagework you do to forward your writing as 'luxuries you cannot, for your creativity's sake, afford to indulge'.

Right now, you are staring a block to personal progress in the face. This block has the ability to stop you. You put the drawing away, or throw it away, and forget about it. Don't.

Hurdle 3

To *wait* is the best thing to do. What form that waiting takes is immaterial. If you already write, you'll know the following procedure well. It's the same one used for a hotwrite.

You leave a piece of new writing for a few days, and you can do the same with a drawing. Then look at it again, dispassionately, in a rather different frame of mind. That always works.

For writing, it works in three ways.

By re-reading a piece of writing you have done you can confirm the following points.

1   You literally 'see it' differently, and that affects how you relate to it.

2   You notice the things that need editing. E.g. The clumsy sentence makes you wince; you turn it around and it reads more naturally.

3   Because this is an open-minded read on your part, and you are not closing down possibility by having *'This is good enough, isn't it?'* playing like a mantra in your mind, you read for development, strengthening and the piece's growth potential. So you see the opportunities to do this.

The waiting concerning a drawing or image happens somewhat differently. The image stays with you and so does the puzzlement concerning aspects of how it's turned out. At this point the way forward again splits into three.

1   The revelatory experience

You may instantly know what this image is about. You may even breathe *'how could I have been so blind as to not see that before?'*

2   The puzzled reaction

The 'no idea' response. It's quite genuine. You have an impression, a vague feeling, but you cannot, as yet, express it properly in words.

3   The dismissive

If you are tempted, at any stage, to say 'it's meaningless' you've just rejoined the 80% Left Brain bias population. This is *Right Brain knocking,* undermining your own creativity. It's a form of self-sabotage, even if you don't recognise it as such right now.

Hurdle 4

If it was revelatory, you may stop there and go no further. Not decode further meanings. Are there further meanings? Yes.

Always? Yes.

This is *wholistic** work, looking at wholes. If you look at wholes from different angles, you see different things. Think of a mountain approached from north, south, east and west. All give totally different views of the same physical landscape. You can guarantee an image will give you at least four different views of one inner landscape of imagination.

You may have to play the waiting game a while longer. The tiny voice that whispers 'it could be...' might offer you something you are not immediately attracted to, so you zap it unthinkingly, in a typical Left Brain move.

Personally, I've found myself going back to retrieve ideas lying dormant in images too often. It's just the Left Brain getting in on the act at a moment you were off-guard.

Hurdle 5

Through time, if you persevere with imagework and its interpretation, you acquire new respect for Right Brain functioning.
You understand the concept of multidimensionality. You more
readily accept the many symbolic meanings inherent in an image, so feel easier and more open-minded about this more creative way of development. You both understand why it works
and have personal proof of it doing so for you. The real value of
doing imagework begins to make a lasting impression. A few
experiences of learning things from self-generated images that
you didn't know or realise previously make a huge difference to
attitude. Remember, the personal unconscious communicates
through the only language it can – images.

If you reach this point, you are well on the way to
having a right relationship between your Right and Left Brain.
The Left Brain serves the Right Brain's creative purpose, and is
happy to take on that role.

Hurdle 6

The organic method offers a natural way to relate to your images.

In writing terms, freewriting is the organic method,
the one used by writers to open up a subject and explore its
meaning. To freewrite on an image's meaning or possible
meaning is a good way to begin this process.

You may well start by feeling inhibited, tentative, unsure. If you accept and acknowledge the feelings yet still keep
on writing, the feelings themselves will change. They may *'mi-
raculously change'* too. Recognise what is actually going on
here. This emotional fluctuation is symptomatic of the Left
Brain/Right Brain power struggle going on in the background.

As more and more meanings occur to you in this
open-minded exploration of your image, the Left Brain will
fall silent and may well stand back and shut up for a good long
time.

However, we are dealing with a lifetime's training here,
remember! The Left Brain is unlikely to give up its habitual dominance easily. The next time you create an image, you may need
to go through a similar inner process again. Don't bother to engage with a dialogue that goes along the lines of the following...

Left Brain	*That was a one-off. It'll never happen again, you know.*
	(Subtext on that is *'I'll do my level best to ensure the Right Brain never usurps itself like that again. I'm in charge here!'*)
Right Brain	*Well, don't you think we should just try. I mean, it was so amazing, so useful, so helpful...*
Left Brain	*Well, if you want to waste your time doing stupid drawings when you are supposed to be writing...*
Right Brain	*Yes. But last time it really worked. You can't deny that.*
Left Brain	*I told you. It was a one off. Spontaneity's the key to creativity. You've done imagery now. You need to move on.*

Crazy as this sounds, remember this inner dialogue comes from a Left Brain bias which each of us individually has to learn to override in our own ways. We writers need lots of strategies.

This inner dialogue is the beginning of role-playing. In assigning Left Brain and Right Brain as individual characters with opposing viewpoints, we engage with inner contradictions. Role-playing increases Right Brain activity, and we will return to consider its importance in creating fictional characters in Chapter 13.

Hurdle 7

A gritty hard-nosed approach to take to decoding images is 'interrogation'. Borrowed from police procedure, it suggests an incisive drive to get to the truth. Even if you don't like the feelings interrogation initially creates, it is worth persevering because of its ability to fully open up Right Brain/Left Brain communication.

Something to visualise
Background on visualisation
If you wish to increase personal creativity, you need to think

and imagine outside the human perspective, the everyday world and the images from homogenised media.

Many different types of energy exist in the environment, some of which humans cannot detect. Animals have anatomical structures that allow them to sense the outside world in ways we have no way of appreciating, *except* imaginally. Echo-location, magnetic fields, electric fields, infrared, ultraviolet and our own five senses heightened and found in extraordinary places. Such as taste receptors on the feet of butterflies and light receptors on the arms of starfish. Elephants hear very low frequency sounds, called infrasound, so have a sensitivity to impending earthquakes.

At the *imaginal* level, writers can use and access these wider frameworks, if it suits their creative purpose to do so.

For the writer, these exercises open doors into the world of creativity. They need to be seen in that way for them to be appreciated as useful.

After reading the following short section, close your eyes and invite a personal response to come to you in the form of an image or images. Veto nothing, from the conventional to the bizarre. Simply accept the image as having a here-and-now relevance and interest to the imaginative Right Brain that you can call on to develop your Right Brain skills.

This is a good level to work at because it is *invitational*.

The visualisation - Superhuman

This visualisation is not about self-aggrandisement or space-age fantasy. As with all exercises, take it at the level that works for you. Under this heading, one writer might choose to change one thing about human beings that would benefit the world. Another writer might choose to imagine a skills-extension that would solve world problems. Breakthroughs in all areas, medical, scientific and aspirational, are located here. These are *first forays*. As a writer, you may or may not wish to go far down these routes, but it's worthwhile taking a look, for both personal insight and creative possibility.

Begin by imaging a human being in some form that represents superhuman to you. Just let an image come onto your inner screen. If it's an accultured one, Grecian god/goddess, Arthurian knight, famous scientist, or current popstar, start there. Let the image change, develop, as it wants to and notice the detail, especially the detail. This is the start of individualisation, making the superhuman your own.

Record what happens in your Learning Journal.

Ways into Image-speak

Step 1 – Go through barrier 1 - draw

Just draw. Anything. Especially if you haven't drawn anything in the last six months, draw. All you are doing is practising putting images on a white sheet of paper. It's an old skill, not a new one. Practising drawing. Reacquainting yourself with a familiar childhood experience. Childhood experience is rich and fertile mind-land for all writers.

Step 2 – Become attuned and sensitive to this act of drawing.

While you draw, feel, and record in your Learning Journal, all those first feelings. Here's five questions to spark your thoughts. It's not a Q. & A. session. Relate to the questions in the ways most meaningful to you. So keeping an eye on it is like watching a thermometer... cold (disinterested) through warm (getting interested) to hot (totally absorbed).

1   When did you last draw?
2   Does it feel different, doing it now?
3   Are you enjoying it, or is it a bit tortuous at the moment?
4   Were you thinking of a writing project, or drawing just for fun?
5   Is there any sense of newness that comes to you as you draw?

7   Begin with your dreams

This chapter on dreams is a journey through its many perceived identities to access a fuller understanding of its potential and usefulness to writers. It's important to review this big picture, and not get caught by the seemingly opposing and differing claims – western culture, experiential, psychoanalytic, dream therapy, native culture, and anthropological. These all result in particular 'takes' on dreams.

These 'takes' must be considered because they influence, and sometimes strongly influence, writers' attitudes towards dreams today. To view dreams as a stepping-stone towards imagework generally is the best way for writers to value and appreciate them.

Mastering the I.D. of dreams

Mastery Learning does not focus on content, but on the process of mastering it. To master the I.D. of dreams to people globally requires you take into account a broad spread of available information, and then set about understanding how it links together. This is a ground clearing activity and necessary to do because otherwise the cultural perception of dreams may weaken any personal resolve to engage with them.

In this chapter, we won't be considering the content of dreams, rather their general attributes. This helps us understand why they are viewed in such disparate ways. Opposite views of the I.D. of dreams is they are 'pure nonsense' or 'source of personal creative power'. That is, either valueless or extremely valuable depending on your viewpoint. Which is it for you?

The multi-identity of dreams

1 *Culturally,* 'pure nonsense'.
2 *Personally,* 'needs an interpreter'.
3 In *psychoanalysis,* a part of therapy work. The founding

fathers of modern psychology, C.G. Jung and Sigmund Freud, held differing belief systems which then reflected – biased - their views on the purpose and function of dreams.

4 In *dream therapy,* the key inputer, the most important thing of all.

5 In *native cultures today,* dreams are viewed as the fundamental connection to the inner power source.

6 *Margaret Mead.* This ground breaking anthropologist lived, for a time, with a native tribe who she rated as the sanest people she'd ever met.   The tribal people spent mornings discussing their dreams.

A New Overview of imagery incorporating dreams

This book is about imagery. Imagery is Right Brain speak. You now understand the value of inner images for creative work. In your dreams, every night, the Right Brain has and uses its opportunity to image-speak. With no interference whatever from the Left Brain which is off-duty for the night while you are asleep.

7 Reasons for writers to do dreamwork

1 Easiest way to learn image-speak
If we wish to encourage Right Brain creativity, the obvious way is to learn image-speak. Not someone else's image-speak, but our own. By remembering and recording the nightly picture-show going on in our heads, we both acknowledge it and tell our subconscious we value it.

2 Welcomes and accepts the bigger 'creative' self
One spin-off to dream-recording and sharing is our tolerance for the bizarre, crazy and wacky increases. We self-taboo less. We inhibit ourselves less. This gently encourages innate creativity.

3 Substantially increases the input of images into overall brain processing
Dreams too are multi-taskers. Practice at recording them not only improves our ability to do so. It improves the Right brain – Left brain links in the brain in the way that best serves cre-

ativity – by starting with a Right Brain image. It also works on changing our habitual brain-balance between image and concept, so we value inner imagery more.

4 Encourages and develops the connection to a personal creative source

Another effect of dream recording is by focusing on image-speak we begin to awaken – or reawaken – that creative power source so well known to native people.

5 Facilitates our own natural image-speak

We become familiar with our own image-speak. We get to know our Right Brains more intimately. We may reach the point where we start to realise some amazing things. By a little nightly practice, we consciously learn the language of image-speak as practised by our own brains. This happens in our heads every night, whether ignored by us or not. It may bring us to ask if it's really so clever to function on half a brain, particularly when the half we deliberately disregard is the creative side.

6 We get to know ourselves better

We may feel we know ourselves too well. This is a Left Brain evaluation, a superficial and one-sided assessment. If we begin to trust the Right Brain and seek its input, help, opinion, view, we will discover our personal 'inner well of creativity'.

7 Dreamwork opens the way into imagework

To zap the Right Brain's offerings is an automatic function of the Left Brain. It's like how we treat email spam. The Left Brain zaps every morning, automatically, as we wake. That reinforcement has been going on all our lives, since the moment we decided dreams were 'pure nonsense'. In all probability, we then continue to categorise them that way. This is an opportunity to take them out of that category.

To ignore dreams is to give them the least credibility possible. To record dreams and work with them opens up your creative self.

How writers work with their dreams

Dreamwork, for writers, performs different functions to the usual cultural ones. The starting point, and the way most people frame dreams, is to want personal dreams interpreted, usually by someone else. At this level, people do not realise or understand the interpretation the *dreamer* puts on the dream is more valid and has more value than any outside opinion.

Dreams are pictures in the mind, dynamic as a personal film show. Dreams have a logic of their own that does make sense once it's understood that symbology is the key to unlocking personal meaning. The same basic process operates in reading or interpreting any image... The Left Brain works in collaboration with the Right Brain through a series of questions to gain a fuller understanding.

Dreamwork, though, carries an added bonus. The Right Brain is not interrupted by the Left Brain. Dreams are the Right Brain's pure-speak. Whether or not we like our dreams or any one particular dream is irrelevant. To encourage all newcomers to dreamwork, relating to dreams using *symbology* rather than *literalism* as interpreter invariably produces lots of new connections. Realisations that actually help us increase our awareness-field. Our inner world grows and expands. This deepens our respect for the sort of knowing held only by the Right Brain.

The double filter on dreams

With dreams, the double filter again tends to block exploration of our inner world through dreamwork.

Strategies of creative writing teachers to overcome student blocks

Creative writing teachers have strategies designed to overcome student-resistance. A favourite strategy is to claim 'personal madness' and then ask the students to 'try something anyway' just to see what happens. As a teacher, to openly call oneself 'mad' in front of a class of adult writing students amuses, surprises and lightens the mood.

The claim of madness is effective in persuading students to give something a go, try something they've never thought of doing. I've watched creative writing teachers use it, admired their skill in handling it and the students' warm response.

I do it in another way. The strategy I favour uses the interactive approach. In writing classes, I get students themselves to find reasons to do any activity or exercise that initially strikes them as having no 'wow' factor in it at all.

It's a step-by-step process. Here's how it works for the task of letter-writing for magazines. This method evolved when one student accused me of *prostituting the art of writing* by asking the class to write letters for magazines. In brackets after each step are written the effects of each step.

Step 1

First, I give the students one sheet of A4 on which are written 50 mini-skills they will be practising by writing letters for magazines. (Immediately they are introduced to the idea of mini-skills and given a very big picture of writing and its developmental and learning potential. Very few people today debate whether writing can be taught, but the 50 mini-skills presentation offsets this view.)

Step 2

Then I ask the students to star the mini-skills they will find personally useful. To choose ten mini-skills. (The students are looking for what's of personal value to them as writers. This encourages them to think about what they need as writers, and order their own priorities.)

Step 3

Next I ask them to share with the group their top three, and tell us why those particular skills are important to them at the moment. (According to Accelerated Learning principles, sharing is the place where the greatest learning occurs. At this stage, the group discovers a lot about each other, their preferences, current understanding and writing aims. This sharing expands their view of what writing means to different people, all of whom want to be writers.)

A condensed presentation which takes students to a place where they see value and personal benefit rather than a waste of time literally melts resistance. It turns the thinking upside down. Now the students can't wait to get started. They give it their best shot. By this method many students achieve publication at the end of their first ten week term of creative writing classes.

These win-win situations are not a selling tactic but an educative one which is enjoyable. Topped with a prize for the student who produces the most letters by the following week it's an incentive to 'go for it'.

That strategy has served me well. In relation to dreams, the obstacles students throw up are different.

Student objections to doing dreamwork

This is a typical student response to the invitation to 'record their dreams'.

Objection: *I don't dream.*

Override: Yes you do. Everyone dreams. Apparently, we'd go mad if we didn't dream. You can have yourself tested if you want. R.E.M. (rapid eye movement) sleep, which you may have seen a pet dog doing, proves you dream.

Objection: *O.K. I don't remember my dreams.*

Override: Leave pen and notebook on your bedside table and tell yourself repeatedly and gently before you go to sleep that you *will remember your dreams.* You have to want to remember them.

Objection: *I've tried that. It didn't work.*

Override: You need to be very patient with yourself. I've been recording my dreams for years, but still I sometimes have to make a big effort to recall them. Especially if life is busy.

Objection: *Yes. I've no time really. Life's hectic right now.*

Override: You need to give yourself space.

Objection: *How?*

Override: Set the alarm ten minutes earlier than usual. You have to give your subconscious many signals that you really mean it. If you have been ignoring your dreams for years, they may need a little encouragement before they believe anything's changed.

Golden Guideline

To turn stumbling blocks into stepping-stones requires we see value in the activity so give it a new priority.

However, we haven't yet dealt with the biggest block of all.

Tackling nightmares

Writers may refuse to have anything to do with dreams – let alone record them – because they fear nightmares. This instant cut-off is best tackled by the self-development/therapy approach, further validated by the experience of the Senoi tribe.

The Senoi tribe took their dreams seriously and were regarded by anthropologists as an extraordinarily well-adjusted, co-operative and peaceful people. They taught their children to stay with the nightmare and to start to take control of their dream-states. (This is the opposite of telling a child to forget about it and go back to sleep.) It's a proactive suggestion designed to overcome the victim-consciousness so commonly found in dreaming in western culture today.

The upfront approach to nightmares advocated by dream therapists is to set up a dialogue between your waking self and the frightening aspect of the nightmare to discover why this part of yourself is trying – and succeeding – in terrifying you.

Key Understanding
If it comes out of your head, own it. Go further and find out what it wants! This integrating move – through acceptance and questioning – will depower and dissolve the nightmare.

Making sense of dreams and dreamwork

Due to the amount of tweaking and reframing involved in bringing together the seven views concerning dreams presented at the start of this chapter, it helps to restate them in a way that connects them up.

The first barrier is literalism. An unwillingness to see or accept the simple fact our Right Brain's language, apart from being a series of dynamic images, also favours the language of symbology. Once again, it's not one filter we negotiate if we wish to understand, it's two filters. We have to decode the picture, and we have to learn to do this using the code-breaker of personal symbology.

Symbology, the language of image-speak and the personally meaningful – once decoded – remains a mystery to millions of people who choose never to learn this personal language.

The popular cultural attitude to dreamwork is 'let an expert tell me'. Two things drive and keep this in place.

1   The publication of books on dream interpretation biases towards outer reliance.

2   Our culture, generally, does not value dreams.

To balance this view, consider its opposite. It is contained in a belief expressed in *Soulcraft* by Bill Plotkin (New World Library, 1-57731-422-0). *Soulcraft* claims we are all searching to rediscover the one image that we were born with. This one image tells us the secret of our life purpose.

Reframing dreams as important to writers

Once we know and understand the real I.D. of dreams, it is easier to understand and appreciate their value to writers. We have to go through this de-tweaking process to factor out predominant cultural influences in order to access dreams' usefulness to writers. Otherwise we never reach a point where we value or appreciate our dreams, let alone learn from them. To treat dreams as a redundant or primitive aspect of our brain functioning, and to demote them as perhaps we do our reptilian brain, denies a large proportion of our natural brain functioning.

The hierarchical brainview which puts intellectualism at the top is still with us, and is likely to remain so unless seriously challenged. Writers are in a good position to challenge that view.

Also, if a person who wants to be a writer uses the outer-world cultural style of thinking as a way to approach and come to terms with the inner world of dreams, it creates a huge mismatch. The inevitable result is a self-imposed taboo on the full use of personal creativity.

Deep imagery work

In learning image-speak, we don't just learn to interpret images for the immediately meaningful. We have to learn the specific symbol-speak that is the unique language of our individual Right Brains. Learning this symbol-speak takes a person into what is today called 'Deep Imagery work'.

None of these appreciations form part of modern education. Modern education prepares people to function in today's outer world. The skills required to do that are often completely different to the ones that give immense personal satisfaction through engaging in meaningful work. The joy of life is not necessarily the daily job; a fact that propels and pushes many people towards writing as a long term career in the first place.

The process of learning

Generally, we master skills by practising them. We become familiar with the practice, and this gives our awareness more space to focus on content – the moment-by-moment experiential aspects. Which can then be further refined.

The I.D. of dreams for writers

1   The hotline to image-speak, the language of the creative mind.
2   Your creative Right Brain's pure voice, unfiltered by the Left Brain.
3   A first contact with personal symbology and its interpretation.

Natural attitudinal changes accompanying dreamwork

We can isolate seven major effects of doing dreamwork which help the writer.

1   Welcomes personal images, values and honour them.
2   An easy way to practise and increase Right Brain image-speak.
3   An easy way to engage with creativity's chaos with its illogical bizarre image-speak. (If it came out of your head as a symbol, it's yours!)

Stated positively, the effect is to make a writer more open-minded. So you don't dismiss something as being mad and automatically taboo it. Instead you are prepared to explore what might lie behind any outside-the-box thinking that's prompted by thoughts prefixed by 'What if?'

4   Strengthens the Left Brain's role as interpreter of Right Brain image-speak. This improves the flow-state between the two hemispheres of the brain. See Chapter 9.
5   Accustoms the writer to 'working from pictures' in a natural nightly way. Mastery Learning remember, focuses on *how* we master new skills, not the content.

Now we move on to the content of dreams.

6   You collect dream data, which you can interpret. Though this data is normally categorised and classified as 'self-development', the activity of dream interpretation deepens and synthesises the inner world, a writer's personal source of writing material and its processing.

7   You collect dream data, which you can use for poems, stories or to generally further your ideas as you learn to trust, more and more, the inner guidance offered by your own Right Brain.

The content of dreams

The content of dreams is unique to every dreamer, reflecting the uniqueness of personality itself. After you have collected some data, in the form of recording your dreams in a Dream Journal, you are in a good position to work with them in an interpretive OR writerly way.

Interpreting dreams

As with assessing any data, the preliminary moves are the same.

1   Identify commonalities, anything at all your dreams have in common with one another.

2   Isolate patterns, patterns of development.

3   Become aware of repeaters; themes, symbols or subject matter.

This gives you a dissociated appreciation – from the perspective of the 'observer in your mind'. This *getting above the subject-matter* helps you dis-identify so you look at your dreams more *wholistically** You are seeking the big picture, and teaching yourself to work in 'overviews', a vital writer-skill.

Writers' use of dreams

The 7-point breakdown of the beneficial effects of doing dreamwork for writers can be summed up through a simple analogy. It's like going to France to learn French. If the ambience is all-French, then speaking English starts to feel out-of-place, inappropriate. By immersing yourself in the image-speak of the Right Brain, you give yourself a similar total experience.

The status of imagework changes from 'weird' to real, accessible, refreshingly new and mine. 'Mine' is very important for any underconfident writer. It's a powerful shift.

The most powerful shift of all to emerge when doing dreamwork is that any absolute claims of logic are challenged. Logic's supremacy and 'know-all-stance' no longer rules. This introduces a flexibility of thinking, a more open mindset, and begins a greater readiness to engage with possibility.

This process is called 'learning to trust your intuition'. It's been favoured by scientists who've made enormous breakthroughs in understanding. Albert Einstein developed his theory of relativity through an inner image which prompted the idea of the curvature of space-time. Today, we are in a better position to understand the power of inner images for anyone who wants to develop their creative potential. Inner images are not confined or restricted to people classified as creative geniuses; they are available to us all.

When you begin to investigate, it turns out images have wonderful credibility.

Something to visualise
Background on visualisation

Dreams offer writers free gifts, creatively, while they rest. These free gifts are an alternative night world, a tolerance for the bizarre, a preparedness to work with and engage with dreams' seeming craziness, plus an imaginal life we could never 'dream up' ourselves when awake. By framing dreams as personal resource, we begin to value them, develop a curiosity for their content and its associations, are intrigued by recurring themes, and start to draw off and explore their creative potential.

The visualisation - Dreams

Colour brings out brilliance, the *wow* and *ahh* factors. The addition of colour creates vivid impressions, easy to remember and superior to rote learning.

Re-imagine a dream you've had, preferably a pleasant or interesting one. Play the dream in your mind as you would a video, but keep pausing it so you have time to make the colours and shapes stand out vividly, more sharply and strongly than in the dream.

Record in your Learning Journal the ease/difficulty of doing this exercise. Use a 0 to 10 scale to monitor it, where 0 is really easy and enjoyable and 10 is difficult and you have to keep bringing yourself back to the task, as set.

This skill relates directly to story-visualising and the ability to slow down your mind in order to big up important scenes.

Ways into dream images

Dreams are 100% images, the pure-speak of the Right Brain. It's only while dreaming this personal hotline is open.

Way 1 – Setting up the Dream Hotline

1   Buy a special notebook and write on the cover 'Dream Journal'.

2   Decorate it if you will. (These are all signals to the subconscious that you now value your dreams. Dreams are important to you.)

3   Make it a habit, every night, to leave your Dream Journal and pen beside your bed.

4   As you fall asleep, tell yourself (gently) you will remember your dreams.

5   If that doesn't work, try setting the alarm ten minutes earlier than usual.

6   Persevere. A bonus is you are learning to favour self-generated images over accultured ones.

7   Increase your desire to remember dreams. (This is an act of will that will repay you handsomely as a writer. Every new way learnt to become a self-starter, self-reliant and inner focused strengthens the writer-part of ourselves.)

8   Record your dream on waking. The longer the gap between waking and writing the less you'll remember of the dream content.

Way 2 – Recording Dreams
Guidelines

1 Record dreams as fully and honestly as you can.
Do not try to logicalise or rationalise them so they
'make more sense'. That's the wrong way to work with
dreams if you want to access their real meaning for
you. Instead, stay faithful to the reality of the dream.
To dis-identify with logic as the ruling parameter,
celebrate the dream's wacky and crazy qualities. (The
process of turning a dream to serve fiction or poetry
is a development.)

2 In your dream-recording, focus on the images.

3 Practice brings facility. Though this process happens
naturally, back it up before sleeping each night by
telling yourself you will remember *more* of your
dreams. Remember, if you are changing the pattern
of a lifetime here it will take effort and perseverance
on your part to do so.

Focus on the bonuses

1 Every time you record a dream, you are banking
inner images and opening the way to self-generated
images.

2 Every time you record a dream, you are working with
the source of personal creativity.

3 Every time you record a dream, you are developing
and encouraging your personal individual image-
speak.

This may feel like a course in re-programming yourself, and that's what it is!

The final bonus...

Participation in and acknowledgement of your inner world,
'getting to know the other half' brings with it a sense of control, acceptance, affirmation, liberation, personal power and
new freedom of thought.

67

Become aware of feelings, positive and negative, associated with dreams and record them too. Favour and value the positive for they will serve you better.

8 Artwork for writers

The variety of mediums, styles & combinations available to choose from in doing artwork may initially excite or daunt, depending on the individual writer. Simplicity is the key to staying focused on the idea of the image serving the needs of the writer who is a non-artist.

Three basic approaches outlined in this chapter give that 'room for manoeuvre' feeling so important to creative work generally. *Doodling, doing what comes naturally and stylised artwork* give the Right Brain writer a competence linked to exploration and development designed to make experimenting an attractive proposition.

Doodling

Doodling has four functions for the writer.

1   It keeps the Right Brain active during Left Brain activities.
2   It's imagery practice, helping the Right Brain/Left Brain balance.
3   Doodling may produce significant images – ones that resonate for the writer.
4   Because it is 'no big deal' it's an easy way to break through any resistance to imagework generally .

To start with though, the word 'doodling' carries unhelpful connotations. Some of the following might be associative for you... *Messing about, not doing what you're supposed to be doing, not paying attention, in another world.* It's frowned upon. Doodling's not exactly anti-social, but it's considered a distraction. It's certainly a distraction if the person sitting next to you is brilliant at doodling and you are having to listen to a boring speaker!

The important learning is this. If looked at superficially, rather than with the intention of understanding what's really going on, we will miss doodling's real point and purpose altogether!

For the writer and those interested in maximising their personal brain-use, doodling's I.D. is very different.

When tested in a lecture situation, the doodlers were found to retain more information than the non-doodlers. However, as with many things in life, when it comes to believing something and taking it on board, nothing beats personal experience.

One Creative writing student of mine was a young physicist already published and highly paid for erudite papers on his specialism. He joined my creative writing class because he wanted to write short stories. While I was talking about short story technique, he doodled. He covered the whole of his file in an intricate web of doodles that astonished the group. His asymmetrical flowing patterns looked – to my untutored eye – like the work of a skilled design artist.

Now include what we already know about imagery being a Right Brain function and we reach a new understanding of doodling's function and usefulness. Doodling is a way to keep the whole brain working in situations where the input – in lecture form – is Left Brain only.

But, like remembering and recording dreams, culturally doodling is discouraged. Yet public doodling, doodling when you are – for whatever reason – in a passive state, helps you not to switch off.

So, in the interests of increasing your personal Right Brain activity, doodle.

In essence, doodling is the baby, embryonic or unsophisticated form of abstract art. There are no standards applied to doodling. No examinations in it, no qualifications attainable. The parameter of requiring expertise, the same parameter that puts many people off doing things, is wholly absent. In status, doodling stands somewhere between dreaming and real image-making.

Reinventing the concept of doodling

Doodling is the ultimate freeform of instant art, often done unconsciously, while the conscious mind is engaged elsewhere. It's an early form of multi-tasking invented by the brain to offset boredom. It's a clear sign you go to your Right Brain to equalise input, and keep your whole brain active.

Here, we've changed the status of doodling from valueless to valuable. We started with its public image as a harmless amusement, signifying nothing except an inability to concentrate. Then moved on to uncover its real and normal function, to keep our whole brains awake in situations where, because of a longish time period exposed to some passive Left Brain activity, we need something to do.

Some people, of course, just love doodling, and that's reason enough to do it.

Doodling for the Right Brain writer
The Right Brain writer doodles deliberately.

1   To increase Right Brain activity.
2   To build a portfolio of images.

As with dreams, prefer your personal interpretations of your doodles. If you say 'my doodles mean nothing' you discredit the Right Brain's input, your Left Brain gets another tick for dominance and you reinforce that 80% Left Brain bias. If you look for meaning in your doodles and are patient with yourself, meanings will slowly emerge.

Doodles offer an easy transition to 'doing what comes naturally', which is the next section. At the cross-over point *doodles* and *doing what comes naturally* merge. Only their owner can decide whether or not they are 'just a doodle' or the beginning of something more significant and important. This is where it's vital to become aware of your emotional reaction to, as well as the visual impact of your embryonic artwork.

In this kind of assessment, remember to bypass 'good' or 'bad' as that's the judgemental Left Brain giving its unwanted opinion. For creative purposes, this critical function of the brain is counterproductive. By slowing down your thought processes, meaning will surface. This Voice of Meaning may be timid, easily silenced. If this is your experience, give your Right Brain a little support and more space to counter the Left Brain dominant mode.

Writer Tip
The oppo-
site advice
concerning
white space
on a page
applies to
the writing
itself. The
amount of
white space
on a page
of text is a
big factor
in how
attractive
it appears
to a reader.
To break
up the text
– use short
paragraphs,
60% dia-
logue, - as
it increases
this white
space on a
page.

White space on a page

If you experience even a smidgen of resistance to the thought of doing a full scale drawing on an A3 sheet, consider this fact. Stateside, the A3 drawing is considered small. In America, Right Brain writers are required to do murals to give full expression to their creativity.

I've lost count of the number of times I've said to students 'fill the sheet of paper with your image'. Then watched as a tiny image appeared in the top right-hand corner – as if desperate to escape off the page altogether!

If writers used the same amount of white space for their drawings as for their text, it would made for a better balance.

Reasons to image big

Aside from the massive boost to Right Brain creativity the big picture offers, there's six other reasons to do the occasional big drawing.

1   For the experience of doing it. To become aware of what it feels like.

2   To honour the Inner child, the one who loved draw ing and colour.

3   The big picture lets you see more, like enlarging a photo.

4   To give yourself lots of room to put in detail which you can later decode.

5   In learning any skill, going 'outside your boundaries' has a wonderful effect. When you return to your comfort zone, you perform better and more easily.

6   The larger canvas invites expansiveness, and is psy chologically liberating.

7   It overcomes the natural initial inertia to doing such a grand performance.

A practical objection is time. To do a big drawing that is personally satisfying may take a few hours rather than ten minutes. The large canvas format is best reserved for a big occasion like the personally important project.

Doing what comes naturally

You may be one of those people for whom drawing is no big deal. Convinced of its value, you may already use drawing as part of and integral to your normal writing practice.

However, this is not the case for all writers. Though you may agree, intellectually, in the power of imagework, that may be insufficient to change long-standing habits.

Often the way to win – meaning to win reluctant writers over to imagework – comes through catching them off-guard. In writing terms, this means approaching the subject from a surprising – yet valid and obvious – angle.

Character-creation from inner child states

Imagine yourself a five year old child again. Really get into this five year old mindstate. It's excellent preparatory work for creating fictional characters. To get yourself in the right Right Brain mode, feel, as completely as you can, the five year old's sense of reality. From the following list, choose the ones that resonate with you and change them to suit your perceptions. Then add your own

1   Just staring. To absorb a world still very new in many ways.
2   A high percentage of surprises in all the learning about the world and the growing child-self's relation ship to it.
3   Sheer delight in doing new things. Experimenting.
4   Massive energy, particularly at bedtime. The sponta-neity that wants to do everything NOW.
5   Curiosity – a desire to explore new places.
6   Excitement – the thrills of doing simple things like playing ball.
7   That smallness that brings flower scents in your face.
8   A love of running, jumping, racing and climbing.
9   Joy at mastery of new skills, like biking and swimming.
10   A fascination with wild creatures or a deep friendship with a pet.
11   Turning anything into a plaything; water, snow, leaves.
12   A highly sense-based appreciation of the world.

Writer Tip
The surprising, unexpected and yet valid angle on a subject is just the technique you need when hunting for a new and fresh approach to a subject for article writing. So you are multi-tasking here; taking down the last barrier to imagework and practis-ing an important writer-skill at the same time.

When you feel fully identified with the this five year old child-state, find a piece of plain paper and some coloured pens and see if drawing takes on a new life for you.

Stylised artwork – an easy extension for non-artists

Stylised artwork puts self-generated images into another framework where accurate representation is not the priority, goal, or even concern. I've talked at length about the purpose and use of imagery for writers as separate and distinct from that of a professional artist. However, these culture-frameworks, the links they embed in our minds, are enormously strong. As we have seen in the preceding chapters, cultural frameworks are a real barrier to any form of thinking differently. With art, imagery and drawing, all too easily cultural frameworks act as a block to experimentation. So the move to stylised art can be seen as an open invitation to try something never previously undertaken. The bonus here is stylised artwork is easy to do.

Stylised artwork's simplicity

First of all, we look at the familiar techniques required by representational artists which are wholly absent from stylised artwork. This reinforces the idea that the usual requirements of artwork that stop the average person from ever picking up a paintbrush in adult life, have no place here at all.

1   *Perspective.* In stylised artwork, perspective doesn't exist. Stylised artwork is two dimensional, not three dimensional as in representational artwork. The concern is not with translating a three dimensional picture or image onto a two dimensional space so it 'appears real'. It's about translating the images in the writer's mind onto a flat medium.

2   *Unimportance of relative size.* At an art class I watched a nearly completed portrait being whitewashed because the relative size of the head to the body was fractionally too large. These sort of frustrations form no part of stylised artwork. In stylised artwork, a so-called 'mistake' can be turned into 'a feature' and may actually provide insight into the deeper meaning of the 'imperfect image'; a meaning not otherwise available to the writer. To take this argument further,

in stylised artwork not only can the relative sizes of real-world objects be ignored, they can be reversed. This offers a new creative freedom.

3   *Unimportance of correct colour.* For most writers, colour-blindness is not an issue. Reframe the parameters slightly and we see that having no colour restriction, like no size restriction, offers a great creative freedom. In that creative freedom lies the power of stylised artwork to really help writers wishing to further develop self-generated images.

As happens so often in any creative work, by going through a perceived block, we turn the block into a stepping stone. The stepping stone here is the ability of stylised artwork to free up writer-creativity in altogether surprising ways.

Common features of stylised artwork

This list of characteristics further reveals the minimalist requirements at the level of artistic skills. At the same time, this list offers a range of techniques that are no more difficult to do than producing a paragraph of good handwriting. The critical voice – the one we are trying to avoid because it zaps creativity – might say 'it's childish, naïve'. That criticism can be turned to a writer's advantage because if a piece of artwork is childish it's also 'do-able' by an adult non-artist.

1   Basic shapes of all kinds. A simplified outline – the sort you'd attribute to a five year old child. Eg A cone could be a firework, teepee, an upside down ice-cream cone or a clown's hat.

2   Lines of dots on a single colour background.

3   Multi-coloured stipple-work as complete infill. It's a colourful way to treat infill.

4   Shapes framed repeatedly for emphasis in different colours. There's a focus and concentration required to do this repetition in ever larger form. It can feel expansive or function as a 'hold' moment. Yet you are still pro-active, drawing.

5   Hatching – criss-cross lines. Hatching is another simple and attractive form of infill. It offers a more open interpretation than filling white space with one solid colour.

6   Patchwork feel created by repeated similar but not exactly the same patterns.

7   Repeated shapes of all kinds in different sizes.

8　　　Outline only of animals/birds/fish. For the really timid non-artist, there's always the option of tracing and cutting out a basic image, then using it every which-way to fill a blank sheet of paper.

9　　　Stick people, Lowry style. The big negative for non-artists is often the drawing of people. Yet a feeling of movement and action can be achieved by using stick people.

10　　　Use of arrows as energy lines. Drawings that use arrows lead the eye in a certain direction.

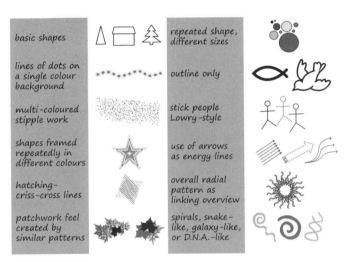

See colour ilustration on page xiv.

1. basic shapes

4. shapes framed repeatly
in different colours

2. lines of dots on a single colour background

3. multi-coloured stipple work

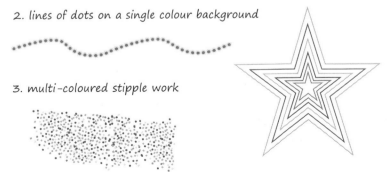

　　　See colour illustrations on pages iii-iv.

hatching - criss-cross lines

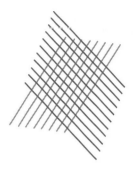

6. stick people, Lowry style

10. use of arrows as energy lines

. patchwork feel created by similar patterns

11. overall radial pattern as linking overview

rapeated shape, different sizes

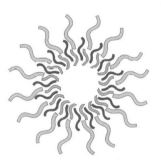

12. spirals, snake-like, galaxy-like or D.N.A.-like

. outline only

See colour illustrations on pages v-ix.

11   Overall radial patterns as linking overview. The radial pattern itself confirms and reflects many Right Brain functions.

12   Spirals – Whatever links you make to the spiral form, its growth associations and dynamism at all levels of existence make it an adaptable and flexible form for the non-artist to use.

Often the first thing noticed in stylised Aboriginal artwork is the dominant image, the one forming the organising principle for the whole piece. The dominant image explored as a multi-sized brightly patterned motif is a good startpoint for a western mind looking for a first organising principle.

Aboriginal style artwork

One of the important tenets of NLP is that by starting somewhere we've never started before, we throw open the 'creative gates' of our minds. To say it differently, not having access to the usual parameters by which we assess and decision-make, means we have to rely on spontaneity.

Earlier, I mentioned that asking students to letter-write for magazines brought strong reactions, in terms of an accusation of prostituting the art of writing. Imagine the level of anger causing such a strong reaction attached to a *different* subject, this time Aboriginal art. The resulting dialogue might go like this. (It's not p.c. But it is an accurate cultural perception.)

Objection: This is tantamount to asking us to become primitive people! In our civilised sophisticated society, this is a step backwards!

Response: You are entitled to your view. Does it change your appreciation to know that aboriginal people have not one, but two meanings, contained within their art? One is a public secular meaning, the other a spiritual one for their tribe. You see, here there's a case to be made out that the aboriginal people, by attaching two distinct meanings to their artwork, rather than just one, are going further and deeper than us so-called sophisticated western people.

Objection: Pah! You'd argue black was white. You are one of those sort of people!

Response: No. I just believe in equality, as originally conceived. Today, there's a realisation that early cultures did and do know certain things which we've temporarily lost. We are now in the process of rediscovering their value and reinventing them for our own use. It's called cross-cultural fertilisation. It's not such a big deal is it?

Going through the unfamiliarity barrier

Blue heart dreaming was my first attempt, several years ago now, at Aboriginal style artwork. My notes about the development of the original drawing (not the graphic design) read:

'It's important to honour your own process, and allow whatever comes to express itself. To NOT impose the conscious mind or take a linear route, but go along with natural development.

1   The swirls of energy in different colours is a symbol I use a lot, the spiral or swirl.

2   Then I added the tree, a pine or root, according to where the line ended.

3   Next came the dotted outline, followed immediately by the blue dotted heart.

4   At this point I got the title.

5   Then came the sand-and-spirit heart bottom and its lines.

6   The triangles came next, and then the dots on all the swirls.

7   Finally the orange horse-shoes, symbolising the need for luck, fortune, good vibes, positive attitudes. Aligning with that, consciously.'

Writer Tip
This is a defuser, designed to take the tension out. In terms of building fictional tension it doesn't. Instead, it strengthens the argument in favour of doing aboriginal-style artwork. Which brings us back on track.

Blue heart dreaming

See colour ilustration on page x.

Wheels within wheels

Seeing with many eyes

Micro-life

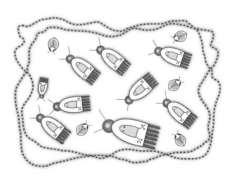

See colour illustrations on pages xi-xiii.

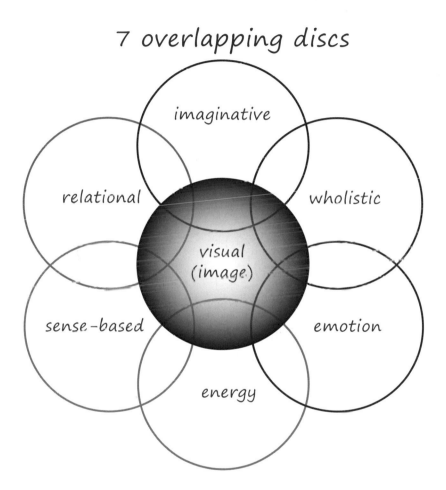

A six – petalled flower

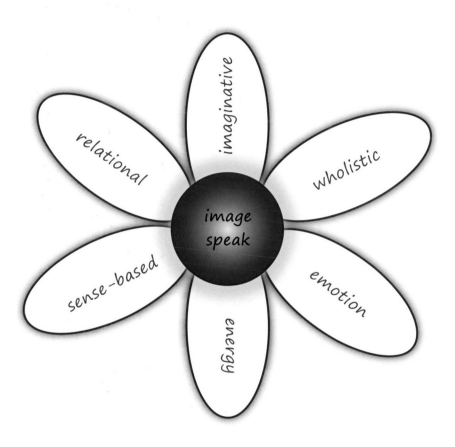

1. basic shapes

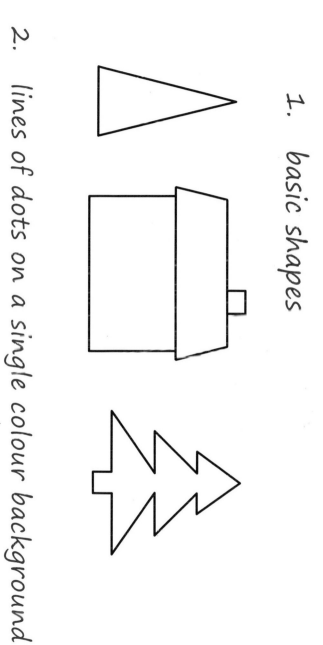

2. lines of dots on a single colour background

3. multi-coloured stipple work

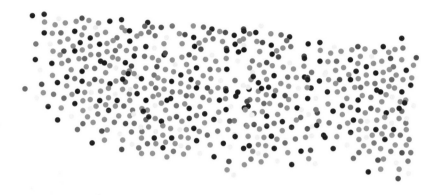

4. shapes framed repeatedly in different colour

5. hatching — criss-cross lines

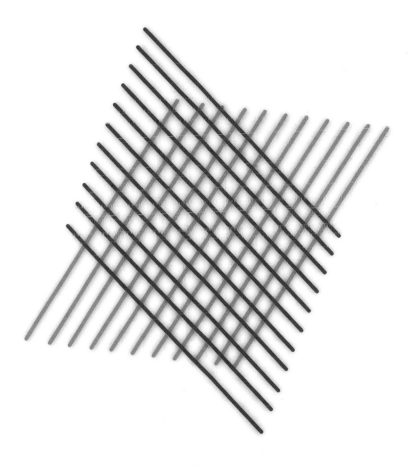

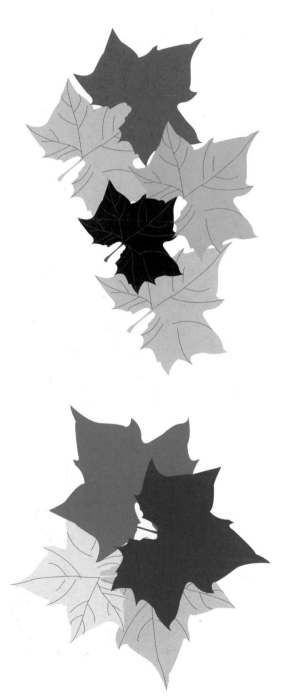

6. patchwork feel created by similar patterns

7. repeated shape, different sizes

8. outline only

9. stick people, Lowry style

10. use of arrows as energy lines

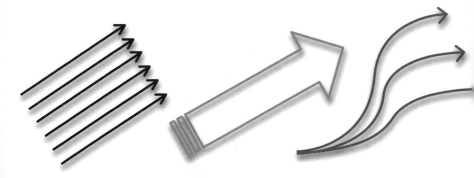

11. overall radial pattern as linking overview

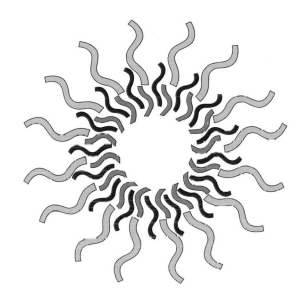

12. spirals, snake-like, galaxy-like or D.N.A.-like

Blue heart dreaming

Wheels within wheels

Micro-life

Seeing with many eyes

basic shapes

lines of dots on
a single colour
background

multi-coloured
stipple work

shapes framed
repeatedly in
different colours

hatching –
criss-cross lines

patchwork feel
created by
similar patterns

repeated shape,
different sizes

outline only

stick people
Lowry-style

use of arrows
as energy lines

overall radial
pattern as
linking overview

spirals, snake-
like, galaxy-like,
or D.N.A.-like

Mindmap of students' "Life is" metaphors

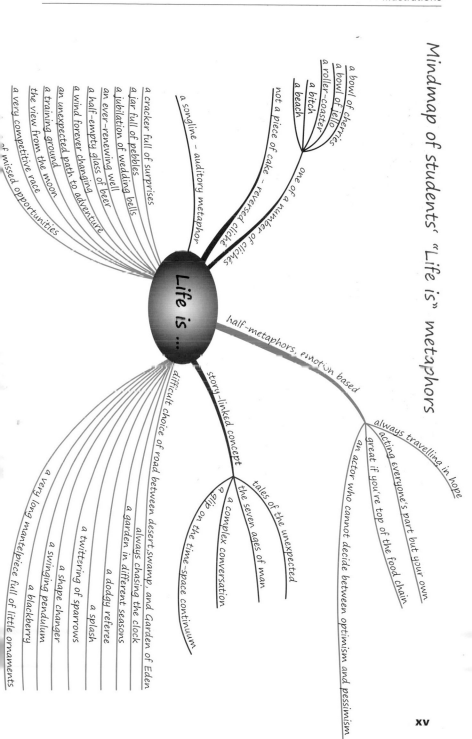

Life is ...

- a bowl of cherries
- a bowl of jello
- a roller-coaster
- a bitch
- a beach
- not a piece of cake – reversed cliché
- one of a number of clichés

- a songline – auditory metaphor
- a cracker full of surprises
- a jar full of pebbles
- a jubilation of wedding bells
- an ever-renewing well
- a half-empty glass of beer
- a wind forever changing
- a wind forever changing
- an unexpected path to adventure
- a training ground
- the view from the moon
- a very competitive race
- of missed opportunities

- half-metaphors, emotion based
  - always travelling in hope
  - acting everyone's part but your own
  - great if you're top of the food chain
  - an actor who cannot decide between optimism and pessimism

- story-linked concept
  - tales of the unexpected
  - the seven ages of man
  - a complex conversation
  - a blip on the time-space continuum

- difficult choice of road between desert,swamp, and Garden of Eden
- always chasing the clock
- a garden in different seasons
- a dodgy referee
- a splash
- a twittering of sparrows
- a shape changer
- a swinging pendulum
- a very long pendulum
- a blackberry
- a very long mantelpiece full of little ornaments

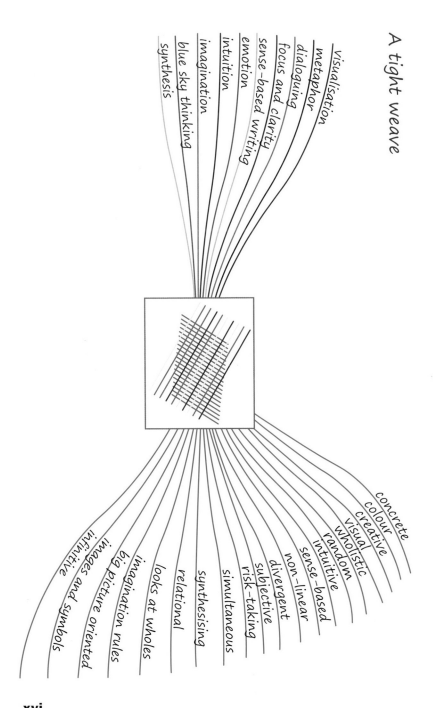

A tight weave

visualisation
metaphor
dialoguing
focus and clarity
sense-based writing
emotion
intuition
imagination
blue sky thinking
synthesis

concrete
colour
creative
visual
random
wholistic
intuitive
sense-based
non-linear
divergent
subjective
risk-taking
simultaneous
synthesising
relational
looks at wholes
imagination rules
big picture oriented
images and symbols
intuitive

These drawings were all done in the spirit of experimentation, with no preconceived ideas. The purpose in doing them was to familiarise myself with the techniques of stylised artwork.

Something to visualise
Background on visualisation

Visualise each aspect of stylised artwork separately. How you could use it. Visualise it, putting your interpretation and distinctive stamp on it. Imagine doing a drawing composed of stylised artwork features. Contemplate how you could combine the different elements.

What do you choose? Where do you go first? What organisational principle do you use? 'Dreaming' is often part of the title of Aboriginal style artwork. Let 'dreaming' lead your thoughts. Does 'dreaming' or the Dreamtime help to bring to the surface of your mind a theme or subject you'd like to explore?

These sort of questions help you to engage with and relate to something that, because of its unfamiliarity, may initially appear off putting rather than attractive. Yet stylised art work is such a basic art-form a bright child at 5 years old could do it. So, if you feel uncertain, invite the 5 year old child you once were to help you.

The visualisation - stylised artwork

Invite onto your inner screen any and any combination of the twelve stylistic techniques. To say *'play with them'* may sound childish, but it's the childlike contained within *toying around with half-formed pictures that come and go in our minds* that works best. It's an inner dialogue... *'What do you think of this?'* You may already practice inner dialogue when trying on new clothes or buying anything where there's plenty of choice. It's assessing with the clear goal of finding something we not only like, but also respond to more deeply. It touches us, excites or fill us with its sense of real potential.

Record, in your Learning Journal, on a 0 - 10 scale, your enthusiasm and/or enjoyment in doing this. Where 0 is less than enthusiastic and 10 is utterly delighted and pleasure filled. More importantly from the learning perspective, record any changes in feelings about stylised artwork, the *'before'* and *'after-doing-it'* takes.

Ways Into Image

Outside of sophisticated representational art, what imagery do you like? What attracts you? This book is predicated on the belief that our inner knowing and preferences are often silenced or overridden in favour of current cultural fashion. We are fashion-tweaked beings. The most important thing for a writer to do is to find their source of personal creativity and follow its development using intuition as principle guide.

Way 1 – Build your personal relationship to artwork

Make a list of the things about artwork you like. Such as, lifts your spirits, creates that warm inner glow, makes you laugh, sends you deeply into gravitas, conveys a sense of richness and meaning beyond that of money, has quality or resonance for you. Consider all art styles from cartoons, animation, to the great masters or so-called primitive art.

For each of your headings, record why. What particular emotions do they bring to the surface? What associations do they have? If this is too clinical an approach for you, write a freeform poem to encapsulate your feeling-state when looking at a piece of artwork.

Way 2 - Doodling

Doodle. Doodle for fun. Doodle extravagantly. Doodle till it is second nature to do it. Doodle till you can feel, inside, its freeing and creative potential. Doodle till you reach the point where it is a subtle mood-changer. Doodle as if it's important and see if that makes a difference.

Way 3 – The big picture

Strangely enough, exactly the same advice applies to resistance to doing a big picture as to an unwillingness to continue with a writing project that has, for whatever reason, got stuck.

It involves a self-question again, but it *works*. That's the point. I've seen disenchanted students arrive at class quite despondent, only to have them go away all smiles at the end of a session. All I did was ask them one simple question.

'What would have to happen here to make you want to do it? 'Do it' being variously translated as 'continue writing the story' as well as 'create a big picture'. For there are certain projects for which people will 'pull out all the stops'. The thing that makes them do it is passion, of course. That willingness to go further, leave the comfort zone, try something new. Initial inertia is the block here, and by now you know what you have to do with blocks. Turn them into stepping-stones. Writers have no choice but to become good self-starters, and this is an opportunity to practice that skill.

By doing a big picture, you are giving your Right Brain a real boost and telling it how much you value its input. Creatively, it's an unbeatable move! Even drawing without initially having a fixed idea of 'what it's about' can be illuminating. To discover, after you've finished a drawing, just how much you understand its meaning can actually be a slight shock. Perhaps this is the moment you appreciate, understand and connect with the quantum claim of Right Brain work. It's certainly a way of going through the unfamiliarity barrier with style!

Way 4 – Stylised artwork

In Chapter 1, we worked on the image/concept balance of the brain, and emphasised the importance of having equal access to Right Brain image or Left Brain concept. Now is the chance to try out this new skill.

Look at the 12 aspects of stylised artwork.

Translate those that are easiest for you to 'get to' into an image in your mind. Deep learning – learning that is personally meaningful – relies on 'making it your own'. The Right Brain does this easily.

Using coloured pens, draw what comes. Refer back to the list at intervals, and incorporate 'what takes your fancy'. Remember this activity is well within the skill range of the under 10's.

You, as a writer, are re-finding an old skill, engaging with it to re-contact Right Brain I.D. and reacquaint yourself with its spontaneity, fun, and the joy of exploration and discovery.

To bring up an inner image, if it helps, close your eyes. Start with a basic image that you can repeat in different ways. At this stage you are not trying to do anything more than re-establish a link with Right Brain image-speak.

In your Learning Journal

1   Doodle whenever you have a few spare moments.
2   Extend your range of stylised artwork.
3   Begin to notice repeating patterns and the effect drawing these patterns has on you. How it makes you feel.
4   Clearly, we cannot translate every image in our heads into drawings. Do a reality check on your image-consciousness generally. Note any changes.
5   Note, especially, if you become more image-aware in other contexts of your life. This heralds a significant change; moving away from an 80% Left Brain bias to a more balanced brain use.

Use these five regularly for a while, and you establish a firm foundation which will make the next steps so much easier. The Left Brain-biased writer struggles with the basic 'show, don't tell' advice given to new writers. (Chapter 11 explores the language and concepts of Creative writing). Many writers never fully overcome the problem. This happens because s/he never understands the role of the creative Right Brain, and continues to expect the Left Brain to supply what it is ill-designed to do.

As with any deeply engrained habit, a highly effective way to tackle the problem or bias is by going to the opposite extreme. For writers who binge on words, (because they love them so much) and 'overwrite', the Image flood in the next chapter is the ideal antidote.

9   Visualisation

Methods to encourage Right Brain functioning

There are many visualisation exercises which encourage Right Brain functioning. The one preferred here, the Image Flood, is particularly powerful. As with any learning, the *doing* is where the real learning occurs. To talk about visualisation is interesting; when you practice visualisation you live it at the experiential level and find out just how it works for you.

The Image-happy writer

A new concept re-orders reality. Consider this. 'Reinventing oneself' gives a *wholistic** appreciation; whereas 'trying something new' suggests a fragment of oneself is getting a makeover. This is an important distinction because becoming an image-happy writer is much more a reinvention than it is an add-on. Your way of processing reality is undergoing a fundamental shift towards a greater involvement of your Right Brain.

The Image-happy writer is the first goal to attain.

The Image Flood

The Image Flood is a 10 to 20 minute visualisation exercise designed to flood both sides of the brain with images. This is a very different activity to watching television, a video or going to see a film. The images flooding your brain are self-generated ones, created by your imagination. There is no dwell-time, no time to embellish, develop or consider detail. It's one flash-image after another. The first time students do an Image Flood, they sometimes have difficulty keeping up with the speed of new picture-formations. But this is a short-lived problem. The brain really seems to enjoy the process – it's fun. The Right Brain responds well to fun. The Image Flood produces a level of expectation and anticipation which keep energies high.

Effects of Image Flood exercises

There are three immediate effects of doing Image floods.

Image floods...

1   Focus attention on the two hemispheres of the brain, raising awareness of them in the visualiser.

2   Are a Right Brain biased exercise, designed to rectify any imbalance in brain use!

3   Have immediate and interesting effects. Students report a heightened awareness of light, greater colour-consciousness and a delightful liberated feeling. Such experiences are stimulating, acting as a refresh to a tired mind.

Two examples of Image Floods

To turn this into an effective exercise, either have a friend read the Image Flood to you while you do a closed-eyes visualisation, or record it so you can play it back later. If you record it, remember to put in 15 second pauses where they are mentioned to give yourself time to visualise.

Sit with your spine straight and your body in a supported and relaxed position that you can maintain comfortably for about ten minutes.

Image Flood Exercise Number One

Consider, now, what you would say to your brain if you could speak to it directly. Apart from 'Hello there', 'wake up stupid!' or 'where have you been all my life?' Instead, assume now is your opportunity to begin a friendship and on-going communication with your own brain that will take your relationship with it to another level.

Close your eyes and focus on your breathing. Allow the rhythm of your breath to become regular. As you do this, allow your consciousness to rest in your solar plexus. Imagine the **solar** aspect of your solar plexus. A personal sun, full of light, heat and energy that gradually moves up through your body, warming, enlivening, illuminating. Feel this personal sun from your solar plexus rise through your lungs and then your heart, moving up the left carotid artery to the left side of your brain. Move your awareness forward now to your left eye.

Keeping your eyes closed, look down with your left

eye. Now up. Look to the left... and to the right. Keeping your awareness in your left eye, allow that eye to circle clockwise... and counter-clockwise. Which direction is easier? You may find it easier if you imagine you are looking at a clock and follow the numbers of the clock as you move your eye.

Now shift your attention to your right eye. Keeping your eyes closed, look down and then up. Repeat this several times. Now move your eye from right to left. Allow your right eye to circle to the right and then to the left, clockwise, and counter-clockwise. Is this easier with the right eye than the left?

Relax your eyes, feeling them get soft and releasing the muscles around the socket. Rest for a minute.

Keeping your eyes closed, direct your attention to the right side of the brain... and now to the left. Shift back and forth easily a few times, noting any differences between the two sides of your brain. Does one seem more accessible than the other?

Keeping your eyes closed and relaxed, imagine the images that will be suggested as vividly as possible. Don't strain as you do this.

On the left side of your brain, imagine the number 1
And on the right side, the letter A...
On the left side, the number 2...
And on the right side the letter B...
On the left the number 3...
And on the right the letter C...
And on the left the number 4...
And on the right the letter D...
And on the left the number 5...
And on the right the letter E...

Continue with the numbers on the left and the letters on the right, going toward the number 26 and the letter Z. You don't have to actually reach 26 and Z. Just continue for a minute or so. If you get confused or lost, go back to the place where the letters and numbers were clearly together and begin again.
(15 second pause)

Rest for a minute, relaxing your attention as you do so.
Now reverse the process you have just done, putting

the letters on the left and the numbers on the right.

On the left, image the letter A...

And on the right the number 1...

And on the left the letter B...

And on the right the number 2...

Keep going toward the letter Z and the number 26.

(15 second pause)

Stop and rest for a moment. Note whether it was easier on one side than the other, whether numbers or letters were more clearly imagined.

Continuing with your eyes closed, on the left side of your brain imagine a tropical beach, and yourself there under a palm tree in relaxed holiday mood.

On the right, image a baby being christened.

Let that image go and, on the left, imagine an annual pilgrimage of devotees to the top of a sacred mountain.

On the right there is a volcano erupting.

On the left is a zooplankton.

On the right is an exploding star.

On the left are new shoots coming through the earth; their tips already tinged red, yellow and blue with the budding flowers.

On the right the trees are heavy with a bumper crop of fruit.

On the left is the sunrise over a misty sea.

On the right is the sunset viewed from a snow-capped mountaintop.

On the left is an undersea coral reef with brilliant angel fish swimming by.

On the right is the Amazon forest.

On the left is a trapeze artist doing a back somersault on a high wire.

On the right is a blizzard.

On the left is the sensation of swimming in warm sunlit outdoor pool. Try to capture the feeling and sensation of the hot sun and cool water on your body.

On the right, imagine how your hand feels stroking a pet dog or cat.

On the left, the feeling of plunging your hands into a

Lucky Dip bran tub at a fair.

On the right, the feeling of moulding clay.

On the left, you are lying in a bath, idly turning the hot tap on and off with your toes.

On the right you are kicking a ball to an excited child.

Now, on the left, hear the sound of a dog barking.

On the right, the sound of a lark singing on a hot summer day.

On the left, the sound of a high wind buffeting your house.

On the right, a recording of Bach's Air on a G-string.

On the left, the sound of an avalanche thundering down a snow gully.

On the right, the sound of feet marching.

Now, on the left, the smell of Christmas cake cooking.

On the right, imagine smelling heavily scented roses.

On the left, the smell of freshly mown grass.

On the right, the smell of a hot dusty city street at dusk.

Now, on the left, the taste of a good mulled wine.

On the right, the taste of hot buttered crumpets.

On the left, the taste of aniseed.

On the right, the taste of honey.

Now, on the left side of the brain, experience as fully as you can the following scene: You are riding a camel through a desert with a container of precious water that is leaking and you are trying to seal the leak with chewing gum.

On the right side of your brain, you are jumping as high as you can to reach a beautiful ripe peach growing on a branch and singing 'Always look on the bright side of life' while being watched by a cockatoo in the peach tree.

Now, eyes still closed, with your left eye look up toward your left brain. Move the eye so that it circles and explores this space. Roam around for a while.

Now do the same thing for a while with your closed right eye on the right side of the brain.

Now, with the left eye, trace some triangles on the left side of the brain. Now make some rectangles. Now make some stars.

With the right eye trace some triangles on the right

side of the brain. Now make some rectangles. Now make some stars.

Now make many overlapping circles on the left side, leaving spirals of light streaming from these circles into the left side of the brain. Imagine the brain as charged with energy by this light.

Make many overlapping circles on the right side with the right eye, leaving energizing light streaming from these circles.

Now, with both eyes, circle vertically just in the middle of the head. You should circle along the corpus callosum, the ridge where the hemispheres of the brain come together. With both eyes together, circle as widely as you can inside your head.

With both eyes, create spiralling galaxies throughout your brain. Fill the whole of your brain space and the inside of your head with them.

Stop and let your eyes come completely to rest.

When you are ready, open your eyes.

In your Learning Journal record:

1   How doing this exercise made you feel.

2   Note any changes in outer perception afterwards.

3   Engage with the exercise in ways that are meaningful to you. E.g. Write about your favourite image, the clearest image, the hardest one to imagine. Note down any surprises and where you feel this exercise was particularly valuable to you. By exploring your personalised response, you are doing the most important learning of all. It will feed directly into your writing in ways that you cannot, at this moment, begin to imagine. Remember 'first times' are the ones that make a deep impression, so spending some time thinking about the Image Flood will enhance its initial effect.

Image Flood Exercise Number Two

As before, sit with your spine straight and your body in a supported and relaxed position that you can maintain comfortably for about ten minutes.

Again, assume you are now beginning a friendship and on-going communication with your own brain that will take your relationship with it to another level.

With today's exercise, at different points, there will be opportunities to make specific choices of image. Try to make these choices for yourself as they occur.

Close your eyes and focus on your breathing. Allow the rhythm of your breath to become regular. As you do this, allow your consciousness to rest in your solar plexus. Imagine the solar aspect of your *solar* plexus. A personal sun, full of light, heat and energy that gradually moves up through your body, warming, enlivening, illuminating. Feel this personal sun from your solar plexus rise through your lungs and then your heart, through your throat to your brain. Move your awareness forward now to your eyes.

As if using a hoola-hoop around your head rather than around your waist, try to make horizontal circles with both eyes just at the level of your eyes. Now circle as widely as possible but inside your head. Then try making smaller circles horizontally at the level of your eyes.

Make them smaller.... and smaller.... and smaller.... until you get down to a space that is too small for circling and then you will want to fix on that point and try to hold it. Continue to breathe freely with your muscles relaxed as you do this. If you lost the point, make more hoola-hoop type circles, then again bring them inside your head. Let them become smaller and smaller until you get back down to a point. Stay fixed on that point for a long as you can easily.

Rest for a moment. Then, in the middle of your forehead, imagine a huge flower of your choice. Then erase the flower of your choice.

Simultaneously, imagine this same flower on the left and some lush green grass on the right. Let them go.

Imagine that there is a big tree growing right in the middle of your forehead. Identify this tree as your tree.

Let go of that, and imagine that there is a musical instrument of your choice on the left, and just a little to the right of it is a drum. Try to hear them as they play together.

Let them go and imagine on the left a bird of prey of

your choice, and on the right another bird, a songster, both of them there together at once. Let them go now, and imagine the songster on the left and the bird of prey on the right.

Let them go, and imagine two birds of prey on the left and two songsters on the right. Let them fade away.

Breathe easily.

Now, in the middle of your forehead, imagine a small sun. Then imagine the sun just inside the top of your head. Try to roll it down the inside of your skull to the inside of the back of your head, so that if your eyes could turn completely around in your head, they would be looking at it.

Now, raise the sun along the back of your head to the top and then down to the forehead. Now raise it along the inside of the head from the forehead back to the top and then to the back of the head, and then to the top of the head and back to the forehead. The sun should be making vertical semicircles on the inside of your skull.

Now let that sun move out in front of you and see it setting over the sea. From somewhere in the direction of the sunset comes a dolphin swimming through the water. From what direction is the dolphin? From the left, from the right, or from some other direction?

Let that image fade away and imagine a giraffe walking. Try to become more and more aware of him as he walks. The giraffe stops and eats some leaves, stretching his long neck to reach a topmost branch. Startled by something, the giraffe breaks into a lope. Then, after a few moments he slows down, walks, and returns to grazing.

Let the giraffe go, and imagine seeing the Earth from an orbiting spacestation. A rocket's been launched from the Nasa base and you watch it approach the spacestation to dock.

You have a choice now. You can either go with the astronauts on an important moon mission, stay on the spacestation doing research or return to Earth.

Having made your choice, let go of that scenario. Let it dissolve completely.

Now focus attention on the left side of your brain for a while. Concentrate on it and try to see or imagine what your brain looks like on the left side. Be aware of the grey matter and the convolutions of the brain. Concentrate in the same way on the right side of the brain. Pay attention to the thick bands of fibres that connect the two hemispheres of the brain.

Now try to sense both sides at once, the whole brain. Sense its infinite complexity, its billions of cells intercommunicating at the speed of light. Meditate on it as a universe in itself, whose dimensions and capacities you have only begun to dream of.

Now, breathing very deeply, imagine that by inhaling and exhaling you can expand and contract your brain. And do this for a while, expanding your brain when you inhale slowly and deeply, and contracting your brain when you exhale slowly and completely.

(15 second pause)

Let your brain rest now and, holding its image, speak directly to your own brain, suggesting, if you wish, that its functioning will get better and better. Suggest that you will have more brain cells accessible to you and that the interaction of the cells and all the processes of the brain will continuously improve as time goes by.

Tell it that the right and left hemispheres will be better integrated, as will older and newer parts of the brain.

Advise your brain that many of its latent potentials can now become manifest and that you will try to work together with the brain in partnership to allow these potentials to develop in your life.

Listen now and see if your brain has any messages for you. These messages may come as words or images or feelings. Give the brain time to respond, withholding judgement. Does your brain want something from you? What does your brain want to give you?

(15 second pause)

Again being aware of the whole of the brain, begin to feel a real sense of both communication and communion with your brain.

Think of it as a new friend and of this friendship as a profound and beautiful new fact in your life. In the weeks to come, spend time nurturing and deepening this friendship so that the two of you (your brain and your consciousness) can work together in useful ways. But now spend a couple of minutes communing with your brain. Images may come to you, or feelings or words, as together you move into a more complete partnership and friendship.

If you wish, while you do this place your hands about half an inch above your head and have the sense that you are caressing the 'field' around your brain, in the same way that you might pat or stroke the hand of a dear friend.

(One minute pause)

If you have some special intention for your brain, offer it now.

Continuing to feel a communion with your brain, open your eyes and look around.

Observe whether there are any changes in your sensory perceptions. How do you feel in your body? What is your mood and your sense of reality? Do you feel that your possibilities have changed? Observe these things.

In your Learning Journal record:

1   Your experience of this second Image Flood.
2   Pay particular attention to any differences, developments, as these signal your own growth curve.

Invent your own Image Flood

This is a particularly valuable exercise as it relates to your specialised interest in writing; sci-fi, fantasy, horror or fiction.

Invent and record your own Image Flood to play back at those times when you feel a disconnection from your Right Brain. That depth of engagement will fast-forward your image awareness, and give you a new versatility and quickness of mind.

Extended Visualisation

Though the five senses were brought into the Image Flood exercise, they need further consideration and a lot more work. Many writers, when talking about visualisation, have a very different understanding of what is meant by that term than ordinary people. For writers visualisation is a total experience, involving all the senses if possible, not just sight. Another way of saying this is *wholistic**, extended or full visualisation.

Extended visualisation is the term we will use here because that's how it feels to the person moving from simply visualising an object or event and faithfully recording their observations – sometimes to the point of overloading the reader with facts – to a sense-based account that engages the reader. ('Engages' means captures the heart, mind and imagination of the reader.)

Though you may not always want to create a full sense-based piece of writing, the ability to do so when required is a major skill.

Here, we are again in the area of Mastery Learning. Acquiring greater control – and awareness of the effect you want to have on your reader – is done by understanding one simple fact. The communication-line you want to keep open between yourself and your reader is Right Brain to Right Brain. To do this, you need to remain as Right Brain as you can in orientation, while communicating through your Left Brain (in words).

At this point you may begin to intuit and perhaps deeply understand why new writers have such trouble with that piece of advice 'show, don't tell'.

What new writers are not told is that they need to stay in Right Brain picture mode, even though the activity they are engaged in – writing – is Left Brain.

The Professional Writer and Extended Visualisation

Established writers often say visualisation, for them, is not just an image. To them, visualisation means *'living it in the mind as if you were living it in reality'*. Professional writers achieve a more exact fit between their imagination and the reality they create and convey through words-on-the-page than does the average person. (Here, too, lies the fascination of fantasy and daydreaming, which are often regarded as the foundation of fiction writing.) Your body is *almost* kidded into feeling as if it's doing what the words-on-the-page conjure, because of the writer's ability to create and recreate feelings, sensations, energy levels, outer impressions, emotions, which make the experience more seven-dimensional than two or three dimensional.

This heightened sensory feast is responsible for phrases like 'getting lost in a book'. The technical term is 'vicarious experience' – as near as you can get to being there without being there. In fact, it's likely if you had been there, you might have not had such a full sensory experience as the one you got off the page. This is because to take in and experience such a wealth requires a perceptive acuity that needs far more time to appreciate and absorb than it takes for the event to occur.

Reality enhancement

In fiction, an exact representation of reality is not what is required. The heightening of key aspects has greater entertainment value. Making things more – particularly more dramatic and intense, or more emotional and gripping, work well. This is why exploring personal feeling-states in relationship to images is so useful. You should find it's easier to link emotion to image than it is to words because this is how our brains are set up to function.

Something to visualise
Background on extended visualisation

In Creative writing classes, sense-based writing exercises are specifically designed to isolate each sense - smell, touch, taste, sound. This helps students focus on one sense only, and deepens awareness of it. E.g. A pitch black night, an unlit passage, or dark cave means loss of the prime visual sense. What is left to the writer is smell - of fire, acid, petrol perhaps. Or touch - as in trying, through your fingers alone, to remember the way forward from a previous experience when you did have use of your sight. Or taste - when in a party game you have to identify, while blindfolded, what you are eating. Or sound - straining your ears to pick up a sound that could indicate a person coming, or a gun being cocked.

The extended visualisation

Choose a sense other than *inner visual* as leader. Sound is a good one because, with your eyes closed, it is easy to pick up and identify a succession of sounds and hold them in your mind. E.g. As I write this, a constant stream of ambient and varied sounds come, of which I am normally unaware. By changing the focus of my awareness to listening, the stream-sound is recordable, second-by-second. *A tiny stone rolling around and tinkling on the conservatory roof, an abrupt hush after a steady wind, a curlew calling way off on the estuary, the many creaks of the conservatory in response to the wind rising again.*

For smell, taste and touch, go, in imagination, to the place and event where each of these senses were, and are, most potent for you. Access the best personal brain-recording you possess.

In your Learning Journal record which is currently the easiest sense to get to, the one most accessible, other than sight. Favour developing awareness for the most difficult sense to capture, so you balance up your senses spectrum.

Ways into Image

The effect of doing Image Floods is to literally open the flood-gate into imagework, and make a writer 'image-happy'. By processing 100 self-generated images in ten minutes, you familiarise yourself with the basic simplicity of the technique and simultaneously begin to alter your own brain balance between words and images.

10 Metaphor

What is a metaphor?

The dictionary definition of a 'metaphor' is 'a figure of speech in which a word or phrase is applied to something to which it is not literally applicable. A thing regarded as symbolic of something else.'

This is a Left Brain description which unfortunately almost completely hides the power of metaphor. 'Life is a bitch' or 'Life is a beach' are both metaphors, but they are clichéd metaphors. A cliché is an outworn expression and needs reinventions to brighten it up.

The writer's most important consideration though is the effect the use of metaphor has on a reader. What metaphors do to readers is put them into Right Brain mode by giving them a picture that instantly 'says it all'. The picture you choose to hand to your reader sets up the writer/reader relationship.

Why metaphorise the corpus callosum?

If we begin with the corpus callosum, we start with a part of our brain we probably never think about even though it is the vital integrating co-ordinating structure which enables Left and Right Brain to communicate. Without the corpus callosum, communication between the two hemispheres of our brains breaks down altogether.

Golden Guideline of Creativity
Anything we think about grows.

Not only do we think about the corpus callosum and all its behind-the-scenes work of which we are normally unaware, we think about it through using a device – metaphor – that possesses five useful qualities for writers.

Metaphor:
- extends a skill you've been introduced to earlier

through the 'image-and-concept' work.

-     is more memorable than using the concept 'a band of fibres'.

-     is a basic writer-skill. The more familiar you are with metaphors, the easier it is to 'pick one out of the air' when you are writing. They come to you.

-     offers an imaginative exercise which targets the personally meaningful.

-     is ideal for introducing the next stage in this process. The metaphor you choose to represent your corpus callosum needs individuation – the personal touch to make it distinctly and uniquely yours.

Writer Tip

New writers often have problems with development. Development of character, ideas, events, plot – anything which requires 'seeing more deeply'. Though interrogation - a method that breaks through blocks through sheer persistence - works, the self-generated image offers an alternative and quantum approach. Immediately, the writer keys into and calls up the full range of Right Brain possibility. To produce a self-generated image (and thereby draw out its meaning for yourself) rather than stay at the visualisation level, you concretise the inner image, further validating the Right Brain's input. Invariably, the result is to reveal still more of the metaphor's potential.

Spontaneous questions arise in the writer's mind. Such as 'What's that?' 'Why have you drawn it like that?' 'And what's THIS meant to be?' (referring to an oddity you were not expecting). These are questions to which the writer may truthfully answer 'I don't know'. What s/he should say is 'I don't know YET'.

Another phenomenon associated with Right Brain work is to find yourself saying something without previously formulating a coherent thought, word or sentence. What it feels like is a moment-by-moment discovery process which your Left Brain can just about keep up with and verbalise as the Right Brain forges ahead.

Writer development

We are going to consider 13 possible metaphors for the corpus callosum. For the new writer the major question is always *'Can I do it?' 'Am I capable?'*

I hold to the belief that every human being is a potential genius. Further, through Right Brain work, the possibility of discovering that *potential* is high.

Later on in the process of becoming a writer, a very different awareness takes the place of 'Can I do it?' This awareness centres on the realisation there are *many ways* of doing it. The writer's chief concern is about making choices. Decision-making at all levels leads the way.

So the 13 metaphors illustrate three things.

a) It's a matter of personal choice. There is no right or wrong, only the personally meaningful.

b) Individuation – the unique development of the chosen metaphor is where the writer 'makes it their own'.

c) The next stage is to find a way or ways in which the chosen metaphor for the corpus callosum can give you more, through time. You plant the idea in your mind that not only is metaphor, being an image, more memorable than a concept; but that its power is set to increase.

You can consider it as the tender loving care that will encourage your brain to give you its best because that's the way you are envisaging it, imaging it and programming it for the future.

The 13 metaphors for the corpus callosum range from the obvious to the bizarre. The writer-explanation for any one metaphor is given to show the qualities mentioned above. That is:

a) Personalisation of any chosen metaphor.

b) How the metaphor is working for me now.

c) How the metaphor will work even better for me in the future. Its growth curve.

Come at this as an academic exercise with no feeling attached to it, and it will never work for you. Giving yourself permission to play, have fun and experiment – the frivolous exterior with the serious underlying intent to discover more about personal creativity – is the mindset you need here.

As well as image-happy, writers need to become metaphor-happy.

In practising aligning metaphors with reality, the writer is introduced to using metaphor at a good level – the personally meaningful one - rather than cut off at the superficial association.

13 ways of looking at the corpus callosum mimics the famous poem – '13 ways of looking at a blackbird' by Wallace Stevens.

13 metaphors for the corpus callosum

These are:

1	Bridge 1
2	Bridge 2
3	A movable staircase, as in Harry Potter
4	Undersea connector
5	Broadband
6	Zany laser beam – like the one connecting Earth and Moon
7	Pair of linked hands
8	A saloon door
9	An athletic tiger
10	A coastal headland with caves
11	Point of meeting of jungle and headland
12	A two-headed dragon
13	A double rainbow, one end in the ocean, the other in land.

Metaphor 1 – Bridge 1

A tiny old stone bridge, picturesque, connecting a recently planted wildflower meadow (representing the Left Brain) with an ancient woodland which has a local reputation for being haunted (representing Right Brain). The bridge goes over a stream where village children come to play in its pools and learn about aquatic life.

Empowerment

a) Connects the new with the old and has free open access to both.

b) The childlike is located at the cross-over point – at the corpus callosum itself.

c) The stream is the ideal flowstate when negotiating the corpus callosum bridge.

Future empowerment

The far-reaching effect is this place is now a Nature Reserve, and there are long term plans to make it better for both wildlife and the visiting public.

Metaphor 2 – Bridge 2

A recent construction, with four levels, one for walkers and cyclists, another for a canal, a third for trains and a fourth for cars.

The bridge has a projected lifespan of 100 years and is a tourist attraction. It connects two countries where different languages are spoken.

Empowerment

a) Multi-access and flexibility of use through a wide range.

b) It's hoped the better communication system will improve relations between the two countries. (The old bridge and its maintenance used to be a cause of disharmony.)

c) The toll – the price to pay to cross the bridge – has gone. It caused traffic jams and frustration. Now it's free access.

Future Empowerment

Two new buildings, like visitor centres, are to be built at each end of the bridge. So new arrivals on each side can become better acquainted with the country they are about to enter, its customs, geography, culture.

With Bridge 1, the writer's concern is with old-new interface, incorporating the childlike and flowstate to enrich its long term future. (Perhaps, too, this writer wants to write ghost-stories! This is a good example of a seed of an idea being contained in an exercise not designed to reveal it, but managing to put in an appearance, nevertheless!)

With Bridge 2, the lack of and difficulty with communication between the two brain hemispheres is now rectified, with both sides making huge efforts to bring this about. (Some writers are far more aware than others of the dissociation between the two brain hemispheres.)

> **Writer Tip**
>
> These two quite different interpretations of 'a bridge' make it clear how easy it is for metaphor and its interpretation to serve the needs of the individual writer, reflect his or her concerns and current brainview. This is the personalised, unique and specific coming to the fore, and empowerment comes to the writer in going through this process.

Metaphor 3 – A movable staircase - as in Harry Potter

The movable staircase links the known world (Left Brain) with the unknown world (Right Brain). The Left Brain is not in charge in this Right Brain world, which is a place of different magical destinations.

Empowerment

a) Seeing the Right Brain as always being a place of magic, discovery and adventure.

b) The excitement of climbing the movable staircase, not knowing till the last moment where it will lead. (Spontaneity is a Right Brain function.)

c) The security of the return to the known place – the Left Brain – and sharing of adventures.

Future Empowerment

Longer trips away will become possible, as increasing boldness as a writer plays a part.

Metaphor 4 – Undersea connector

Supplies and transports enormous amounts of energy and electricity contained within and protected by a strong pipe on the seabed.

Empowerment

a) The energy flow to the Right Brain is important because it's been completely cut off in the past.

b) Minute quantities of electricity are part of human brain functioning, so there is a grounded link between brain and undersea connector.

c) It's out of sight, not intrusive. The only person aware of the huge change in brain use is myself.

Future Empowerment

Bringing light, heat, power, energy to dreams I thought I'd lost is something I'm really looking forward to doing.

Metaphor 5 – Broadband

There's a miraculousness about the optic fibre, just as there is about the micro-chip. The enormous potential of something so tiny, blink and you'd miss it.

Empowerment

a) Broadband's carrying power is the quality I want most in my writing, that multi-access facility. All channels open and available at the touch of a computer-mouse, or the lightning thought.

b) Instant means nothing is far away and 'difficult to get at'. Or muddled, or vague, or woolly.

c) Because it's not a question of having to have a bigger brain, just use my own interior computer more efficiently, this feels really empowering.

Future Empowerment

The connecting-up that this broadband corpus callosum will bring is a completely new sense of identity. That'll take a while to get used to!

Metaphor 6 – The Moonbounce

The Moonbounce takes on average 2.55 seconds to make the return Earth-Moon trip of 380,000 km.

Empowerment

a) Distance, speed and the laser beam's intense narrow beam suggest enormous single minded power, and that's what I need.

b) Power to go the distance is more of an issue for me than contacting my Right Brain. But I feel that if I become more open to my Right Brain generally - which means a radical shift in brainview – I may well find the real solution. It's the wavering light – the swing between high and low motivation that stops me.

c) The moon as Right Brain accurately reflects my reliance on it. I need to remember the thin sliver of a moon, the crescent moon, is just an illusion.

Future Empowerment

To contact the full moon of personal creativity at will, that's my goal.

Metaphor 7 – Pair of linked hands

This image changes constantly. One moment it's the handshake, then two lovers holding hands, then hands together in prayer. It insists on being all three at once

Empowerment

a) The handshake is the bond of trust – as well as being a formal greeting. I go with the bond of trust, developing trust between my Left and Right Brain. No more power struggles, I now know when it comes to creative matters, my Right Brain is in charge.

b) Two lovers holding hands is trust as well, but at a deeper personal level, one they both hope will last a lifetime. My Right Brain as a stranger to me yet, whom it will take me a lifetime to get to know intimately.

c) The prayerful moment, the spontaneous, almost pleading gesture people sometimes make. It's the opposite of a demand, has more in common with a courageous hope; an openness to possibility and potential.

Future Empowerment

Now the image becomes one, all three together, present simultaneously. That is its most powerful expression, when it combines and contains its maximum emotional impact.

Metaphor 8 – A saloon door

I'm not happy with this, but it's the image that came. As we've been asked to explore what comes I thought I'd go with it and see what happens. I'd certainly never have thought of a saloon door! It came as a full blown image, the complete wild west scenario!

Empowerment

a) Pioneering in this strange land of the Right Brain, a frontier land where you make up the rules as you go along.

b) The freedom to be myself and going through that saloon door I know I'll meet many other like-minded people. Perhaps they are fictional characters waiting for me to bring them to life.

c) It is a door anyone can go through, to a place of rough conviviality, where emotions run high, and survival is a real issue. Thinking about it, that saloon door puts a grittiness into life I personally respond to rather well.

Future Empowerment

To set up a new life for myself is an option I've toyed with in the past. I really think it's only a matter of time before the symbolic in this image becomes reality for me.

Metaphor 9 – An athletic tiger

Tigers are athletic anyway, but this one has a fantasy level capability.

Empowerment

a) It's about going over obstacles. The bigger they are, whatever they are, the higher I have to jump. From a domestic situation which crowds me to a block in my writing. Really, that's the way it is.

b) As a free wild animal, there's an extra dimension to this tiger though. It's his spirit.

c) It isn't fantasy at all. It's an automatic reaction. It's willpower.

Future Empowerment

This has been my way of dealing with life since forever. But this tiger is not one I'll ever forget because he incorporates so many of the qualities I personally admire and know work. Courage, indomitable spirit, and now I have inbuilt a special ability to get into my Right Brain instantly.

Metaphor 10 – A coastal headland with caves

When I started drawing this, I hadn't a clue how it was going to relate to the Right Brain/Left Brain connection at all. In fact, I didn't think it did.

Empowerment

a) The headland is the Left Brain. The caves represent the Right Brain because they are hidden, deep, and have many secrets no-one has yet discovered. The caves are also linked by passages. It's a complete network, whole in itself.

b) It's when the tide comes in, bringing the flowstate, the creative juices really waken up. But there are deep pools in the caves, so it doesn't matter that much when the tide goes out.

c) This metaphor is about bringing what's hidden in the caves out onto the headland; from the Right Brain dark into the Left Brain light.

Future Empowerment

It may become quite a famous area actually, attracting lots of tourists, once the caves are fully explored.

Metaphor 11 – Point of meeting of jungle and headland

The jungle is the Right Brain, the headland my Left Brain.
Empowerment
a) A jungle is a mixture of things; adventure, discovery but also holding terrors which, if I rush into it, may catch me out. I really want to explore the jungle, but the corpus callosum is my compass so I can find my way back to the headland.
b) The compass is my inner orientation, which will keep me on track. It's intuition really, and I am a very intuitive person. So that fits well.
c) Now I know the link between the two, I'm really happy to go exploring this jungle. I can actually feel excitement at the prospect.
Future Empowerment
It's the compass again. Knowing that my intuition is going to be deepened, extended, developed in ways I cannot possibly imagine right now – that's so personally empowering.

Metaphor 12 – A two-headed dragon

The Welsh legend of the two dragons fighting is intriguing.
I didn't expect it to turn up as a metaphor for my corpus callosum though!
Empowerment
a) I remember my delight at finding that dragons did actually breathe fire, just as electric eels give you a nasty shock.
b) I like the idea it's one dragon though – that unity. It's only at the head there's two, the Red-head my Right Brain, the Green-head my Left Brain.
c) Full co-operation exists between these two because I've been a writer for a long time. It's good to have confirmation the Red-headed Dragon is still in charge though!
Future Empowerment
As this was a completely unexpected image, I take it as a sign I need to court inspirational fire a little more in all aspects of my writing.

Metaphor 13 – A double rainbow, arcing from land to ocean

The land represents my Left Brain and the ocean represents my Right Brain. This feels appropriate because the land, generally, is solid, mapped and known. The sea is both shallow and deep, transparent and dark, and even today contains much that we are only just beginning to learn about.

Empowerment

a) The double is important. The major rainbow is the big link, the one operative throughout all areas of my life. The fainter rainbow is any current writing project I'm working on at the time.

b) It's not just an overarching link, the colours are important. They give me a balanced perspective, which allows me to see 'many viewpoints'. It's not that I will never be biased or opinionated, but the rainbow enables me to get above my personal concerns and view my life dispassionately.

c) The land and sea representing Left Brain and Right Brain feels right, empowering and informative. I need to be reminded regularly of the huge difference in functioning between the Left and the Right Brain. The land-sea analogy clearly signals the totally different ways the two hemispheres of the brain function.

Future Empowerment

Rainbows aren't there all the time, and their absence will nudge me into remembering I have to put them in place myself when thinking about my personal creativity.

Debrief on the 13 metaphors for the corpus callosum

The ad hoc off-the-wall quality of these responses is absolutely in keeping with what happens when writers open themselves to the potential of metaphor. When they start to trust the metaphor to tell them a great deal more about their inner motivation and needs than any concept. The uniqueness of such personalised interpretations ensures memorability.

Whether the metaphors are naturalistic or man-made in orientation is not important. What is important is the honouring of the image that comes to mind in response to the idea of a metaphor standing in for the corpus callosum.

You may have noticed that some of the metaphors offered seemed a little off-centre; more about willpower, the identity of Right and Left Brain or an honest self-evaluation than focused on the connector between the AR-tistic and logical sides of our minds. The jungle metaphor went even further away from the exercise as set. The writer not initially realising her corpus callosum acted as a compass to help her re-orientate if she got lost in her Right Brain jungle.

This seeming lack of focus is quite in keeping with how the Right Brain and creativity generally, operates. It isn't actually lack of focus at all. The Right Brain is more likely to address the needs of the person at that time through offering an appropriate image than directly answer a Left Brain question.

Workshopping with corpus callosum metaphors

When work-shopped, this metaphorising of the corpus callosum exercise is done differently. In pairs, participants are asked to work up ten potential empowerments contained within each of their chosen metaphors. This kind of expansion happens naturally when doing group work.

The exercise works on two levels. Apart from being excellent metaphor practice, it encourages students to focus and refocus on empowerment which is great for confidence and learning to 'think differently' – in N.L.P. style. The diversity of interpretation shows how it is possible to make 'anything work for you', in the sense of turning it to your writing purpose. Here we touch on another Right Brain skill – the flexibility of thinking that arises from a divergent, random, intuitive, imaginative and relational approach.

Something to visualise
Background on visualisation

The chapter itself is the preparation for this visualisation of your corpus callosum in its most empowered state. The many associations students have with metaphors cannot be predicted in advance. A writer's personal associative network is unique. Associations, being subjective, are Right Brain, drawn up from personal life history and life experience. *Yours is more valid than any you have read about, simply because it is yours!*

The visualisation - Corpus callosum

Play with the corpus callosum metaphors. Let your mind move over them without attachment to any one of them. Can you, by imagining the corpus callosum as it really is - a thick band of fibres, - then fuzzing that image, draw up a metaphor that feels appropriate for you?

Remember to adopt an *invitational* approach to this exercise but at the same time be patient, accepting and prepared to 'hang on in there'. If you haven't given real credibility to your Right Brain's offerings for a long time, the first job is to re-establish contact. The second job is to encourage a freeflow of images.

Ways into Metaphor

Choose one way of the four listed below. Ask yourself a second question to focus on it more... What are you most comfortable with as an on-going metaphor for encouraging greater freeflow both ways across your corpus callosum? What feels right to you?

Way 1

Invent your own metaphor for your corpus callosum. Draw what you visualised in the last section. Discard all the metaphor suggestions offered in this chapter. They've served their purpose. They've opened your mind to possibility and, more importantly, potential and development.

Way 2

Pic 'n mix. Take some aspect or feature you like from the metaphors which attract you. Consider what your own brain feels like. It is possible to become aware of its background activity and how it supports our everyday life.

Way 3

Choose just one of the listed metaphors that you feel you can 'get into' right now. There is no point in taking on a metaphor which does not feel relatable in some way, even if it is exotic and rather exciting. The purpose of this exercise is to find a metaphor you can live with.

Way 4

It is, of course, possible to reinvent the corpus callosum every day using a fresh metaphor according to how you feel. If you choose to do this, don't neglect the deepening developing aspects, because they are key to getting the most of your material when it comes to forwarding writing projects.

Whichever way you pursue doesn't matter that much. Just ensure you have:

a) An image that's a metaphor for your corpus callosum

b) Three points why it's an empowering metaphor for you.

c) A feature about your empowering metaphor that is getting more, better, greater, stronger, daily. (Try using a fantasy element to really extend possibility, and your imagination.)

11 More on Metaphor

Throughout this chapter, I use expressions visual, kinaesthetic and *metaphorical* where possible to illustrate the difference this makes to the feeling-state and sense of aliveness within the writing that is then handed to the reader. These are expressions that major at the level of image and action. The deliberate choice of, and preference for, feeling-state words and phrases over concept-based ones conveys flavour, tone, mood, angle and approach of the individual writer. The place inside yourself you are writing from reflects the highly animated state that marks doing creative writing exercises for enjoyment, boldness, fun and sometimes to be deliberately outrageous.

An example which fulfils these parameters is the *'Life is...* as a metaphor' exercise.

Nine ways the 'Life is...' metaphor works

It offers the opportunity to:

- explore imaginative and intellectual frameworks
- reinvent a worldview
- deeply root into own nature... say who you are.
- reconsider underlying beliefs against a much expanded and colourful pallet of options.
- play devil's advocate.
- play for its own sake.
- explore a field of ideas not previously entered or considered.
- reveal gaps in thinking.
- open up a whole range of new scenarios.

The *'Life is...'* metaphor as a writing exercise - 7 benefits

For the writer, the *'Life is...'* metaphor offers seven mini-skills. This should come as no surprise, as Right Brain input is present throughout this exercise, contributing at many levels to encourage creativity. The *'Life is...'* metaphor offers seven ways-in, all present at the same time, so fulfils the 'simultaneous' nature of Right Brain learning. In *wholistic** terms, it's a catch-all exercise.

1 Mindmapping as a writer tool.

Tony Buzan's mindmapping methods have been with us for many decades now and are still being developed today. The mindmap as set out on the page with the key word in the middle is a visual invitation to search for meaning in all two-dimensional directions.

2 Cliché-weaning

Clichés quickly emerge when doing this exercise. Immediate cliché-emergence mirrors writing-process too. Until we are cliché-weaned, or develop a natural aversion for such hand-me-downs, a cliché often comes to mind before an original metaphor.

3 Reinforces image-concept distinction

Somebody usually says 'Life is what you make it' or 'Life is difficult'. These are concepts. No image comes to mind and, with so little to go on from these blanket statements of reality, they don't work.   By dealing with and eradicating concepts at the start, there's less likelihood of reverting to writing off a concept rather than an image.

4 Big picture oriented

It's an opportunity for students to see the whole playing field at once. When developing ideas, a mega-overview is not automatically the start point unless we choose to make it so. Many people, writers included, naturally access what's important to them and stop there. Mindmapping *'Life is...'* reveals wider perspectives.

5 A balancer of viewpoints

The downbeat cliché *'Life is a bitch'* is immediately countered by *'Life is a beach'*. This initial downside-upside take gives the negative and positive poles and invites students to play in the metaphorical territory in-between.

6 Right Brain sourced

In Right Brain terms, the 'Life is..' exercise is fun, imaginative, creative, image-based, random, spontaneous and often involves most of the Right Brain functions. Colloquially, it ticks all the boxes. As with metaphorising the corpus callosum, there are no right or wrong perspectives. What students choose to explore is just that. Therefore, it is a repeatable exercise in future years to monitor change. Change in belief, attitude, imaginative growth, confidence, boldness, belief in image's power and metaphor's ability to exceed personal expectations; the place of startling discoveries.

7 Mindmapping for future projects

To witness how well a method works, to see it in action, acts as a great motivator to use it again. Most people today are familiar with mindmaps but may not fully realise their potential for writers. Metaphor-based mindmaps deliberately bias the mindmap towards image rather than concept.

Mindmap of students' 'Life is...' metaphors

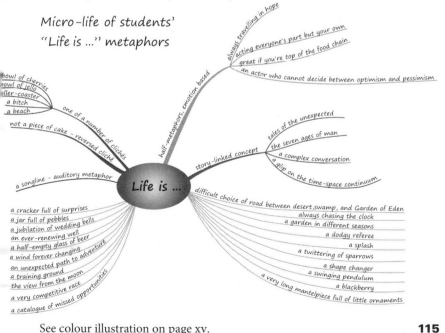

Micro-life of students' "Life is ..." metaphors

always travelling in hope
acting everyone's part but your own
great if you're top of the food chain
an actor who cannot decide between optimism and pessimism

bowl of cherries
bowl of jello
roller-coaster
a bitch
a beach
not a piece of cake – reversed cliché
one of a number of clichés
half-metaphors, emotion based

tales of the unexpected
the seven ages of man
a complex conversation
a blip on the time-space continuum
story-linked concept

a songline – auditory metaphor

Life is ...

difficult choice of road between desert, swamp, and Garden of Eden
always chasing the clock
a garden in different seasons
a dodgy referee
a splash
a twittering of sparrows
a shape changer
a swinging pendulum
a blackberry
a very long mantelpiece full of little ornaments

a cracker full of surprises
a jar full of pebbles
a jubilation of wedding bells
an ever-renewing well
a half-empty glass of beer
a wind forever changing
an unexpected path to adventure
a training ground
the view from the moon
a very competitive race
a catalogue of missed opportunities

See colour illustration on page xv.

Ways to interpret and relate to this mindmap

These metaphors are student originals. As such they accurately reflect students' perspectives at various stages of their learning.

Classifications and categorisations are Left Brain tools that don't necessarily serve the creative process. Does it help to distinguish *dynamic* from *static* metaphor? Or *positive* from *negative* metaphor? It depends. I believe it is more useful to wait and see what a writer does, subjectively, when developing - through a ten minute writing exercise - the metaphor they've drawn up from their personal associative network.

The classifications I've superimposed on this student mindmap are meant to distinguish a full visual metaphor from its near-relations; half-metaphor emotion-based, auditory metaphor, and story-linked concept. These distinctions are useful to writers because they open into other writerly possibilities of development.

The only criteria I've used to give the metaphor a big tick is the presence of an image within it. Read and interpreted for individualistic take, these metaphors provide a series of image-statements that suggest a questing for personal meaning.

The 'Life is...' metaphors produced by students are quite as diverse as the ones that emerged when metaphorising the corpus callosum. This indicates the infinitive Right Brain field at work, big picture oriented and divergent.

Many creative writing teachers use the random-concrete-visual mix of Right Brain functioning to kickstart imaginative exercises. Here a different trinity of Right Brain attributes is used. Because the 'Life is...' metaphor starts with the wholistic* big picture, it invites students to stand back and take a long look. It invites them to reflect on their own lives and address a big question to access a personal worldview. That worldview may then be coloured in different ways according to the writer's temperament and angle of attack – witty, horrific, off-beat, wacky, ironic, or clever and insightful.

The 'Life is...' metaphor may reveal to students things previously unacknowledged. If they are unused to doing Right Brain imaginative work, it will certainly open up their awareness of what it's possible to do. This exercise opens a door in the mind. Having taken a peek, it really is then the student's choice whether or not to go through that particular door into their creative world.

At moments of personal dissociation from a project, story or poem, it's helpful to remember that current emotional feelings are not as reliable a guide to action as is the main driving force of your personal life. This is where the *'Life is...'* metaphor may score because it can reveal a centre. An aslant approach to this centre may help you to see *Life* in an entirely new way.

The willingness to try things, even if they are not initially attractive, seeds an open-mindedness which, yes, will sometimes lead to dross. See 'failure' or 'not working' as a step on the road to 'breakthrough'. You just need to learn to use the Right Brain to help you. And call on Albert Einstein's *'willingness to stay with a problem longer than usual'* as back-up.

Teaching yourself to cultivate an open mind is a background and back-up writer-skill. If you have been writing for a long time, it's likely you know the experience of feeling not a single spark of enthusiasm or energy for a long project. Yet, if you turn your mind to it, embrace it, give it your attention, introduce some new associations you hadn't considered before, it will spring to life and give you unexpected developments. Work with it. Wrestle with it. Hang on in there.

The not-quite metaphors

Included on the students' mindmap are certain *'Life is...'* expressions not strictly metaphors. i.e. We don't get an instant image. Yet we only have to look at where they are leading to know that, for a writer, this is a good place to go. They are not closed-ended concepts (Left Brain) like 'difficult' or 'what you make it'. They might give you an image if you worked with them, brought your personalised take to them to find a mind-picture that led on from the statement. As an example, for *'Great if you're top of the food-chain'*, do you get dinosaur, eagle, whale or man? Similarly, '*a complex conversation*' needs interpretation but its associated meanings... *relational, character-based, dialogue-rich,* is fertile ground for any writer to explore. *The Seven Ages of Man* is concept not image but its rootedness in overview (Right Brain *wholistic**) gives it a certain credence.

You might be tempted, as I was, to categorise according to the inherent negative or positive within the metaphor. Bypass that.

Useful Learning from the 'Life is...' metaphor mindmap

What may first occur to you on considering the *'Life is...'* metaphor mindmap is *'how individualistic they all are'!* The people who suggested these metaphors have associations with them that you and I might never guess.

Some, like *the view from the moon or an ever-renewing well* have a certain authority and universality. They speak to us all, though these two metaphors work at different levels. The view from the moon gives the home we all share. *An ever renewing* well offers a recognised perception of creativity's I.D.

This exercise opens up worldviews, and the opportunity to reconsider worldviews. It leads some students to take control and make changes to move towards a more desired *'Life is...'* metaphor. It can also seed ideas for stories, an angle on a subject not thought of before, or even a poem. The appearance of *actors* twice in this mindmap of metaphors could indicate a budding playwright or a Shakespearian influence that is seeded as of now and will start to grow into the creation of great story characters. The creative in us has no truck with logic. To pursue the associative connections is far more fruitful.

A glip on the time-space continuum is a concept but it earns its place on the Metaphor mindmap because of its originality and story-making potential. As does 'tales of the unexpected', which suggests open-mindedness, readiness for and expectation of change, the unpredictable and divergent upfront.

The literalism within a metaphor can offer a humorous image. As with someone who is literally *'chasing a clock'* (see Chapter 12). We may feel some of these metaphors lock us out. That our own minds are incapable of reading any real meaning into the metaphor. We may find ourselves exclaiming in exasperation 'How?' That over, we may start to feel curious. What connections could be set up, for goodness sake, to make a *blackberry* mirror life? Did someone really say that?

Remember, here, you have to work hard to give automatic leadership to your Right Brain. The Left Brain is ever ready to ridicule, scorn, or put down.

Working with half-metaphors

Half-metaphors are ones where there's a vague image behind the words, or the potential for there to be so. But it's not concrete, definite. It's often tinged with emotion, the subjective, so hooks into Right Brain are present. With just a little more consideration – possibly whilst doing the writing itself – an image will come to mind.

Startpoints into the 'Life is...' metaphor

There's three areas students come from when they engage with an exercise like this.

1   The personal reactive. The likely source if a person's life is pressured. Then writing becomes a release, therapy, *the chance to let it all hang out.*

2   The considered. The possibilities of a wider framework override purely personal considerations. An objective attempt; a detached viewpoint that lets us 'see more' carries its own rewards; we grow in understanding.

3   The imaginative or playful. The place of boldness, experimentation and fun. Humour-based and sex-based contexts make writing more memorable; saleable and entertaining. One function of the writer is to entertain. Some writers cannot resist the land of double or treble meanings and innuendos. It's as if writers are magnetised to ambiguities.

A personal choice of metaphor can draw on any or all of these impulses. That choice determines the start point, suggests the tone being set up and the focus of the piece. Sometimes writers work *across* their chosen Life metaphor, engage it in a dialogue, and become oppositional to its perceived public I.D.

'A *dodgy referee*' indicates the one in charge is not quite up to the job, or has personal agendas working against fair play. Whereas '*a training ground*' may not touch on or question this aspect. Or indeed, postulate anyone being in charge. The commonality, the Game of Life, will be treated quite differently by writers developing these two metaphors.

When learning metaphor's scope, writers don't just access the whole new language of image-speak and their personal Right Brain creativity. They underwrite their conceptual base with dynamic pictures which they can decode.

Extended metaphor - exploring metaphor's potential

The subsequent ten minute writing exercise gives students the opportunity to explore their chosen metaphor. Find the place it excels; dazzlingly reflects their feeling-state. Locate the place where it hobbles and goes lame. The metaphor no longer holds up. It breaks down, becomes a cul-de-sac. We have to retrace our steps, try another angle.

This is a first foray into the realm of Extended Metaphor... To find out how far a metaphor can be pushed before it breaks down. After extricating oneself from the dead ends, to find what new associations it sparks. Ones more fruitful, which have 'legs' as the most prolific British stage playwright, David Campton, used to say. *'Will it run?* Is it going anywhere? 'To mindmap a personal *'Life is...'* metaphor is another depth-dive into imaginative possibility.

Extended metaphor as cliché reinvention

Bright witty articles thrive on this, where something stale and too well known is given an upbeat or cynical twist. The writer is then able to key into a kind of universal shorthand - where everyone knows the original meaning and are delighted to see it getting a makeover. This happens when we writers look at things aslant.

E.g.

Life is a beach until you meet the quicksand.

Life is a bitch on heat with the dog-pack after her.

Life is a bowl of jello where the wobbliest bits taste best.

Life is a bowl of cherries floating on a wine lake.

Life is a roller-coaster where the thrills ahead keep beckoning.

Note: The image is retained and developed to either reverse, balance or extend original meaning.

Writer Tip

Playing with metaphor-extension is excellent preparation for the sort of article-writing that requires a definite viewpoint – for, against, or slant. A piece where success does not depend on choice of words, a secondary consideration. Success in writing viewpoint articles depends on the primary consideration – strength of argument. And that relies on developing a network of mind-links as support system. Where the logical mind says 'context-jumping', the imaginative mind says 'metaphorical link'.

So this is about teaching yourself to operate in ways which extend rather than limit your imaginative range and thinking field. Additionally, to want to go there for the individuality it allows us, as writers, to access and express.

Example of extended metaphor as a poem

A simple illustration and example of an offbeat take on extended metaphor is a published poem I wrote called '*Life is a blackberry*'. Here, we'll consider its structure and not its poetical qualities, which are rather obviously wedded to rhyme and metre. Here we are talking about the fruit not the phone.

Life is a blackberry

Life is a blackberry waiting for you
Unknown as black, bright as sundew.
Small as a bullet, hard with it too,
mangled, fly-eaten, bitter right through.
Or full to the bursting, it bleeds at your touch
giving its all too soon and too much.

Life is a bramble, that is for sure,
a challenge to find us out evermore.
It tempts us to folly, stings us to pain,
then invites us to do it all over again.
It stays out of reach, so clearly in view,
it dazzles our eyes and we plummet anew.
When we fall to the thorns, a blackberry we meet
It was sitting right there, all the time, at our feet.

Juicy with dew from summer's long quest
Its low place means nothing. It's one of the best.
Yet the high one we find is not nearly so fine
as when we first glimpsed it up there in the sun.

Delusion dressed up in a fruity disguise,
An autumnal joke full of surprise.
Not just for the jams, jellies and pies
but to help us live life and smile at its lies.
Ready to show us the way back to earth,
to alter our thinking, question the worth
of all that we see and all that we hear
in gathering in the fruits of the year.

This poem's invitational start compares fruits with life-polarities. The first stanza makes the direct metaphorical link to life-situations and this is sustained to the end of the poem. The background activity of the experience of going blackberrying when young followed by mothers transforming the fruit into delicious food grounds the poem is a reality known to children, even today. i.e. The poem is accessible.

The poem is a journey from seeing, wanting and picking the fruit to eating it in its transformed versions. It focuses on the picking – on the 'doing it' and how that mirrors and feeds into life-experience. As such, it reflects the native American belief in nature as teacher; something I did not know about when I wrote the poem.

Something to visualise
Background on visualisation

From this chapter, it's rather obvious that metaphorising life takes individual writers in unexpected directions, as in divergent, non-linear, intuitive, imaginative, creative and sometimes, risk-taking. The effect is to reinforce the perception that the right way is the way that is right for you, courtesy of your Right Brain!

Naturally, metaphorising life, the corpus callosum or anything else, if done in a group situation, pushes the individuals taking part to 'come up with something', even if they are not wholly happy with their chosen metaphor at the time.

There's three stumbling blocks needing turning into stepping stones here.

1	The new writer honestly does not realise the wealth of Right Brain potential waiting to be tapped. Of course, by now, *you* do!
2	The new writer doesn't like an initial image or idea and abandons it altogether. The more prudent tactic is to record *something*, which s/he can return to and develop later when in a more receptive frame of mind. Otherwise, that first seed is lost.
3	The new writer is, unwittingly, unknowingly mentally lazy.

The 'Life is...' metaphor is a mega opportunity that may give you a lifeview so informing and enriching it provides a new focus and even a self-reinvention.

The visualisation   'Life is...'

View this 'Life is...' visualisation as a warm-up for the 'Ways into Image' section that follows. As reader, you have one advantage over students who are working within a time-limit; you can experiment more widely before making a final choice.

Regard this visualisation as a preview, and hold the expectation that this will allow you to focus up your final image more clearly. E.g. Say you chose 'Life is a dawning' and visualised what that means to you as of now. Later, when you did the 'Ways into Image' section, this then became 'Life is a dawning when the shutters are open.' That's a more focused development.

Visualise your 'Life is...' metaphor in the spirit of it being a preview.

Ways into life metaphors

Outlined below are three routes into a 'Life is...' metaphor. They are not three separate exercises, but three distinct ways of thinking about it. Go with what works for you.

Route 1

Try this ten-minute writing exercise for yourself. Do not be concerned if your *'Life is...'* metaphor doesn't quite hold up, express, fulfil or do justice to your feeling-state. The important thing is to explore and experiment and be bold in doing so. If further associations occur to you after you've finished a ten minute write, take this as a clear sign you are on the right creative track. The analogy of *'peeling back layers of onion-skin'* as a way to reveal more, describes the creative process very well. The act of recording your first thoughts simultaneously clears the mind and stimulates it to produce more associations. Having good ideas at inconvenient moments is a natural hazard in a writer's life. Just keep your journal with you if at all possible. Say an encouraging 'yes' to every offering your Right Brain gives you, and it will give you more still. It is about going further into your ideas. It's also about building reliance – belief and faith - in inner knowing, and the only person who can do that is YOU.

Route 2

People respond differently to creative writing exercises. Some 'need lots of handles'; some get the idea straightaway and cannot wait to get started. These people change places too, and the 'inspired' one week, is the one who is slow to take fire in another session. The important learning is to accept these moods and the brain's variability in response. Acceptance is often the easiest way to unblock the creative in oneself. So Route 2 is a little more prescriptive, but may open a window when the door's locked.

The structure of the poem quoted *'Life is a blackberry'* can help start you into metaphor.

1   Find the polarities within your chosen metaphor and you will define a playing field, the area you can explore.
2   Find the personal, the place where you connect deeply with the metaphor.
3   Consider how the metaphor functions in the real world and the links and cross-overs into human mind-states and experience.

4   Add one fantastical element, a *'What if...'* to raise the level, strengthen the parameters and give it more punch.

Route 3
The Sporting Analogy

In sports training generally, people are encouraged to go outside their limits, play against and with those far more skilled than themselves as a way to raise their game. The bonus is when players return to their usual level afterwards, they bring with them a facility and ease not previously possessed. They are now playing well within their boundaries and this boosts confidence. The 'spare' they feel at playing at their familiar level contributes to their overall enjoyment of a game. It can even contribute to becoming more spontaneous.

Think of this depth-plunge into metaphor as just that. A chance to become, not blasé about handling metaphor, but doing it with a boldness beyond your 'normal'. Put that patina on this exercise and your future writing will benefit from the associative bridges you are building into panoramic views of the possible.

Writer Tip

Metaphor has great credentials in linking the creative mind to the kick start expression that needs to flash brighter than any commercial advert for a writer... *'What if...'* Every time you use it, 'What if' can act as a catalyst to move the mind away from the obvious and into the personally meaningful.

12 The language and teaching of Creative Writing

This chapter has two foci – the language and the teaching. As in the medical profession, the first part of this chapter demonstrates how we tend to treat the *symptoms* rather than the *causes* of writing problems or ailments. The second part of the chapter looks at and compares seven learning styles favoured by teachers of Creative writing.

Concepts used in teaching Creative writing

Three concepts familiar to all involved in creative writing and its teaching are 'show, don't tell', 'make a scene of it' and the kinaesthetic injunction concerning best-sellers – 'words should jump off the page'.

Metaphor is not the only Right Brain way of handing an instant picture or image to your reader. Analogy and simile do the same job, and are ways of 'giving students handles on process'.

This constant movement and crossover between literalism and symbolic meaning might seem confusing at first. But that only happens when you think superficially. Once it is understood what's going on beneath the surface – the setting up of a Right Brain to Right Brain communication and connection between writer and reader – this problem disappears. Once again, we meet a now familiar pattern – the importance of having equal access to both image and concept in your writing and thinking. To develop brain-balance, and improve your writing, not only favour images, but become aware of them and whether their 'automatic presence' is now increasing. Are pictures, images, metaphors, similes and analogies becoming a greater part of your thinking round and brainview?

Natural break

Put a percentage on your current image-concept ratio. Is it 30% images, 70% concepts? Can you achieve, even for short periods, an 80% image-base to your thinking? Better still, have you control over where your thoughts are coming from – in the sense of Right Brain or Left Brain? At a moment's notice, can you switch to academic mode, and couch everything in concepts? Then imagine talking - on the same subject - to a bright 5 year old, (whose young mind can only comprehend the world through pictures) and fill that young mind with a memorable meaningful moving image?

Show, don't tell

This basic concept wonderfully illustrates a deep underlying problem to do with creative writing and its teaching.

An analogy serves to illustrate this more vividly. If we treat the symptom rather than the cause of the problem, the problem will persist. A symptom of something being wrong in our bodies is physical pain. My physiotherapist has to deal with many people who just want the pain to 'go away'. They would rather take pain killers than take exercise, develop an atrophied muscle or change the way they move their bodies. So the underlying problem never goes away.

The underlying problem in the teaching of creative writing is that it is a Left Brain approach to teaching a Right Brain skill. Showing is Right Brain, telling is Left Brain. If a writer has already produced an image, they are more likely to stay in Right Brain mode, or find it easier to do so, than if they are working in Left Brain mode only. To tell students to 'show, not tell' doesn't work very well; sometimes it doesn't have any effect at all. Models, examples, of 'what we mean' go some way to showing students what's possible. But it is all too easy to erroneously conclude that you are 'not creative' when the truth is the Right Brain skills have not been activated.

To return to the analogy of the physiotherapist, we stay at the surface of the problem (the words on the page) and neglect to look or pay attention to, the underlying cause, (using the wrong side of the brain as creative source).

Make a scene of it

An easy way to explain something new is to start with what people already know, so they have a jumping-off point; a place that's already familiar and they are comfortable with. The concept 'make a scene of it' is one such easy route into understanding what is wanted. Contained within 'make a scene of it' are drama, exaggeration, over-emotionalism. 'Making a scene of it' even has another meaning to do with personal behaviour; that someone is making too much of it, altogether overdoing it.

To invite new writers to 'make a scene of it' can be a liberating and enjoyable experience, the 'letting it all hang out' of student description of the I.D. of creativity. In story-terms it is just what's wanted – the emotional dwell-time, the dramatising of an event, considering every detail from a sensual perspective where taste, touch, sound, sight, smell are heightened. All these give an extra emotional dimension and connection that plunges a reader into the fullness of Right Brain appreciations.

'Making a scene of it' is a visual construct, implying something out of a film or soap opera. 'Making a scene of it' is a shorthand concept based in a thoroughly appropriate image we all understand. Therefore it definitely earns its keep in the creative writing lexicon.

Words jumping off the page

I first heard this expression from a lecturer who was talking about writing best-sellers. It was just before the invention of the concept 'page-turning quality'. The language used to talk about creative writing has evolved alongside all language use: another writerly one is 'character-based plot'. Character-based plotting means what happens in the course of the story tests the character because of the kind of person s/he is. It's an invitation to look at either the weakness of a character or any obsessional tendencies s/he has. Then to make sure the story action tests the character at these points where s/he'll feel it most and it will most matter. This guarantees a strong emotional motivational basis, the emotion used to bind the character and the plot together. Using these parameters to work up a story ensures the potential is there for a powerful deeply involving story.

'Page-turning quality' is not so easy to deal with because there are more factors involved. 'What happens next?'
clearly relates to 'page turning quality'. 'Words jumping off the
page' doesn't but were this lecturer's way of trying to convey to
an audience of writers qualities such as empathetic characters,
urgency, tension, drama, gripping excitement, a thousand per
cent reader involvement - or any other invented overblown
phrase that means total immersion in a story.

Consider the expression 'words jumping off the page'.
It's a kinaesthetic image, one based in physical movement, so
this lecturer may have had a natural kinaesthetic bias, rather
than the more common visual or the less common auditory
one.

For a moment we need to focus not on what the lecturer meant, nor her natural method of processing reality but
the *image* that comes to mind. Alphabet gym? Which letter
jumps highest? Words jumping over one another, leapfrog
style? Jumbled up letters all arriving back on the page in a
meaningless heap? Total desertion, and a blank page! (So the
reader turns the page to see if there's any words on any pages?)
The logical follow-through does not hold! I'm not being face-
tious here. It's only by looking at what results from *not* basing
creative writing in the creative side of the mind that we end
up with such a ridiculous and inappropriate image that cannot
take any audience to the heart of the matter. How much simpler and easier it is to say by sourcing your creative work in the
Right Brain, you automatically access images galore, emotion
and the full range of sensual experience.

Anecdotes- right Brain mini-stories

Anecdotes, little stories, are Right Brain because they are
personalised (subjective), and encourage the listener to live
through the event (a vicarious experience) with the storyteller.
Some people, even today, communicate more in anecdotal
form than through direct speech. They 'storify' everything that
happens to them.

Many years ago (another version of 'once upon a time')
I was a student of a well-known Scottish writer who taught at

Glasgow university. At the start, like a zealot, he absolutely insisted on 'show don't tell' as one of the most important writer-skills to master. Over several decades, this total insistence on 'show, don't tell' changed to a recognition and belief in two sorts of writers... 'show writers' and 'tell writers'. What caused this fundamental change of appreciation?

The modified position did come with one stricture... the 'tell' writer must use a high percentage of dialogue. Today it is as much as 60% dialogue to text. This high percentage of dialogue helps readers to retain the illusion 'they are living through the experience with the characters'. To say it differently, the 'showing' is still present, but relying on the medium of dialogue only, rather than sense-based writing.

If the 'writing fashion' hadn't changed from the old 30% dialogue to today's 60% dialogue, this writer-teacher might never have changed his viewpoint.

Another likely influence is, of course, that work in an academic environment encourages conceptual thinking. If a person is not aware that the whole argument is actually about brain use – from which hemisphere we source our writing then debates end up discussing personal preferences rather than come from the deeper understanding about how we have been educated and taught to think and value brain functioning. We see either/or situations – as in either show or tell – rather than using both, as and when appropriate.

Strange results appear from over-valuing Left Brain functioning. Highly educated people may learn to show, but still feel the need to tell as well. So their writing slows down, the action stops as the writer takes us through an event twice. First by telling us what happened, followed by a showing section to give us the same event close-up and personal. This style of writing is appropriate for lecturing or non-fiction writing – tell them what you are going to tell them – then tell them (or in storyform, 'show' them), then tell them what you have already told them. It obeys the Rule of Three so well-known to advertisers. Generally, for something to be learned, remembered, people need it presented to them at least three times, each time in a different way.

It is extraordinarily hard to wean people of patterns

in their writing. They may be completely unaware of these patterns because they are totally focused on words. Patterns and patterning tend to be a Right Brain function, but is one of the brain functions which can reside in either brain hemisphere.

When people start writing, words themselves can take on an all-consuming quality. Initially, this makes it difficult for new writers to get to things like overviews, saying in one sentence what a piece of writing is about. Another related problem area is focusing up the balance of a piece, - what to emphasise and explore deeply. Or even where there's need for a short connective passage to ensure seamless prose.

Being in love with words has a downside... Generally, readers don't love words as much as writers do. Readers get impatient with what used to be called 'purple prose' - long descriptions which they often skip. Readers want to know what happens next. Which is why writing teachers often start with the very thing they know is likely to get missed out... the action. It's an effective way of redressing the balance. It leads straight into action images, the subject of Chapter 15.

How to deal with early mismatches

Some confusion is unavoidable in any learning process. Yet anyone can gain insight by looking at their current thinking style, how it's influenced by their education, job, training and career. Then decide where the biases are likely to be and begin to take control. This means isolating what you need and need to practice in order to advance certain writer-skills. As is rather obvious by now, many of those skills are sourced in the Right Brain.

The English language as writer's artistic medium

This concept keeps us attuned to Right Brain image-speak. To present the English language, or any language, as a writer's artistic medium isn't said to metaphorically over-egg the pudding - enrich the meaning beyond the bounds of common sense. It's said to remind ourselves of the next logical step in a sequence which began with valuing and revaluing imagery.

The English language has the largest word-base in the world; it is a word-supermarket, with thousands of options available courtesy of a dictionary. We can often find ten words that more or less fit our intended meaning. This word-richness pushes writers working in the English language to consider exactly what they want to say and how they wish to convey it. This occurs at the same time as they keep a sharp eye on the direction the piece is taking. This overview encompasses where it's come from, where it's headed and whether the linkage throughout is sound. With a strong Right Brain source, quantum in nature, these functions are simultaneous.

Word-culls

In the drive for exactness and succinctness of expression – the advice to aim for economy of words – word-culls translate into losing adverbs and adjectives and persuading verbs and nouns to carry the precise meaning the writer required. For example, 'very' is very suspect. 'Very good' may well do better at conveying the intended meaning if called 'excellent'.

Repetition of meaning is another red light area, and often slips by those who are less observant. To *ascend vertically* doesn't sound out-of-place, yet it's repetition. Interestingly, an adjectival or adverbial style often hides the writer's desire to express something more strongly or fully. For this service, s/he'd do well to employ metaphors.

It's not a wholesale adjective/adverb cull that's needed. The adverbs and adjectives that escape this word-cull are those that alter or *make more specific* the meaning of the upcoming verb or noun. Such adjectives and adverbs are doing an important job, focusing up the picture behind the writing. For example, consider to hop *sideways*, to fly *downwind*. *Sideways* and *downwind* are adverbs that give specificity to the verbs *hop* and *fly*. With the examples of a *deserted* battlefield, and a *silent* spring, the adjectives *deserted* and *silent* change the meaning of the nouns *battlefield* and *spring*.

The adverb/adjective cull – also called 'losing the modifiers' - works well at the mundane level. It's a level a writer must attend to nevertheless, if s/he has publishing aspirations.

Writer Tip

For a meta-
morphosis
of language,
to turn it
from a fac-
tual account
to an easily
imagined,
felt and
experienced
reality, you
cannot do
better than
rely on
metaphor.

Reframing in action for the writer

For the new writer, communication is paramount. Does it make sense? Do we, the readers, follow? The move from writing for oneself to writing for a larger audience is rather like moving house; things are in different places. What, subjectively, makes perfect sense to you may not to your reader, who hasn't your mindset, your associative network and interests, or your personal history which has formed your opinions and outlook on life.

For the creative writer, the movement from individualistic to universal, from subjective to a more balanced appreciation requires you never lose sight of your imagined reader.

The English Language – its downside and upside

Sadly, though the English language offers the greatest word-base in the world, it is often not allowed to show this potential. This is because of the need for 'ease of communication'. Writers are warned off using words that are not in the common lexicon. Poets and those writing in a more literary style are often exempt, but the insistence on catering to the least educated, has contributed to what is today referred to as 'poverty in the use of the English language'. Certainly, we use a restricted pallet, as research projects into the average word-base of various groups of people, has proved.

The upside is to be found in the abandonment of obsolete words that no longer describe or address our cultural reality. The word-cull of the obsolete results in room being made for new concepts, phrases and expressions, to which writers themselves are free to contribute. A reinvention of language moves us away from cliché, helps us become more aware of our personal language use and what we can do with it to help us say, literally, new things. Things never said before.

It is important for writers to know this background to the current state of the English language.

Word-deconstruction is often revelatory. 'Understand' still works well. As in 'getting under the words to see where this person is standing, coming from'. Other words fare less well. Butterflies used to be flutterbys. Flutterbys is a far more appropriate name than the image conjured by half a kilo of chilled flying fat unexpectedly sprouting wings.

Can creative writing be taught?

This question used to be hotly debated when creative writing classes first started. Though it seems a simple question, it isn't. It depends what is being taught. But it is also possible to ask 'what do students want from Creative writing classes?'

Seven Learning Styles

1   The Model System based on personal success.
2   The Prescriptive system – what to write.
3   Lecturing
4   The Model system based on published work and student interest.
5   Tasters
6   The Creative System – interactive workshops.
7   Accelerated Learning / Right Brain techniques, as outlined in this book.

Importance of What is Taught

Even the words 'teach' and 'learn' imply a different focus. The first is teacher-based, the second learner-based. Learning is the most important.

There is natural overlap between some of the seven systems. *Lecturing* may easily take the form of an hour's talk about personal success. *A Tasters term* attempts to cater for the full range of writing interests, and links easily into a *Model system* based on published work and student interest. *Interactive workshops* are a forerunner of *Accelerated Learning.* The reason to give them space in this book is to put imagery and Right Brain methods into the larger context of what Creative writing is about.

At the brain-use level, here we need to consider the Right Brain's big pictures, the synthesising of connecting it all up, and identifying new links which give further insight. This is just the sort of process which happens with any material when developed. We're using creative writing as an example of how this works but also to clarify and explain why students sometimes display strong negative reactions to speakers / lecturers / tutors in Creative writing.

What the new writer gets from each of these systems.

1   *The Model system based on personal success*

Chiefly, it's inspiration, the chance to rub shoulders with a literary great. How entertaining it is depends on how good a speaker – as opposed to how good a writer – the author is. Take your Learning Journal so you can doodle.

2   *The prescriptive system – what to write*

Unless this is flagged up as a specialised course, say in writing short fiction for women's magazines, a highly prescriptive approach often raises people's hackles. They intuitively feel there is little room for personal creativity when they are handed too many instructions.

3   *Lecturing*

It depends on the academic level and the overall purpose but lecturing, with its 30% content retained – remembered – is not a great way to learn. Take your Learning Journal so you can doodle and get the most out of it.

4   *The Model system based on published work and*
        student interest.

This system incorporates published work and moves towards the interactive and student-based by asking participants to bring extracts from favourite authors to class. It's a Left Brain method but is student-led so offers more opportunity for that all-important sharing and interaction.

5   *Tasters*

A flexible approach which appeals to many students because of the dip-in, dip-out quality. One week they're doing playwriting dialogue, the next week poetry. Such a mix is stimulating, and a good way for newcomers to try out various genres and writing styles.

6   *The Creative system – interactive workshops.*

Spontaneity, and the off-the-top-of-your-head quality to group-based work fast-forwards ideas and thinking.

7   *Accelerated Learning/Right Brain techniques.*

In a group workshop situation, the diversity of drawings and their interpretation is mind-expanding. Accelerated Learning claims to be 300% more effective than conventional learning.

So which of these will best serve your purpose? What do *you* want from a Creative writing class?

I always ask students what they want from a forth-coming ten week term, and often they have no idea. 'To see what it's all about' is unfortunately sometimes as good as it gets. A vagueness of purpose is not good for writers. It indicates they have an expectation the teacher will inspire them. Which is fine as long as that's viewed as a kick start and doesn't become a permanent. At some stage writers need to transfer their inspirational needs to their Right Brains. All writers need to be or become self-starters. To pursue this line of thought one step further, we might ask, Are writers who attend creative writing classes primarily social writers? Has Adult Education fostered and nurtured groups of people who prefer Writing Classes to Writers Circles or groups? Are creative writing classes consid-ered more serious and academic and therefore less fun?

More importantly what sort of group is most likely to produce writers of the future?

This is no idle question. It's one posed in a slightly different form by Colin Wilson - who wrote the fifties best-seller '*The Outsider*' (Tarcher, 0874772060). In his book about writing '*The Craft of the Novel*' (Ashgrove Publishing Ltd. 1853980064) Colin recounts his experience of lecturing to stu-dent writers at an American university. He asked them:

'*Who is going to write a best seller then?*'

None of the students raised their hands. Colin fol-lowed up.

'*If not you, then who?*'

There are no definitive answers to these sort of ques-tions. The only point in raising them is to show, for writers, the initiative, choices, lie wholly with them and within them.

If we listen to poor models we are in danger of emu-lating them, because we think that's all there is and they are the experts. Put this against the Mastery Learning route and we come to realise that once we've mastered basic technique, the way forward is to take control of and change the way we use our brains. One expression is '*power up the brain*', which makes sense if we become aware we've over-relied on just half of its full functioning capability.

The way to use your brain to deeply tap into personal creativity can certainly be taught. With the added bonus of balancing the brain's natural functioning on the way.

Something to visualise
Background on visualisation

As writers, we respond positively to different imaginative triggers. And respond positively to different triggers at different times. But the full picture is more complex. By going further we writers gain more in all areas related to creative process; more awareness of possibility, more ability to stay with an idea, and, more faith in the process to give us what we want from it.

Consider Walt Disney's perennial take on the creative ideas of those who worked for him. *'We know this idea is good. Now, in what ways* (not way, not the hunt for just one elusive thing) *but **ways** could we make it great?'*

I now know that, if an idea doesn't have fire for me, it's because I haven't yet found the parameters - parameters personally meaningful and universal, that will speak to, interest and hopefully fascinate readers.

The visualisation - Alphabet sport

At the kinaesthetic level, visualise - by s-t-r-e-t-c-h-i-n-g the letters, - the letters themselves physically doing their chosen sport. Does such an image instantly communicate?

That's the warm-up. Now imagine a letter of your choice, give it a sport, and visualise it as fully as possible, doing all the moves associated with that sport.

Record what happens, paying particular attention to the moments when your chosen letter felt most 'alive', the image at its strongest, dynamic or humorous.

Ways into learning
Way 1

Record a time of significant learning experience for you. What made it so memorable? Be honest. If an important factor was 'a gorgeous teacher with a great sense of humour', say so. If a deep desire to pass an exam was the motivator, say so. If a passion for the subject overrode all other considerations, record that. Exploring your personal learning 'triggers' deepens your awareness of what presses your learning buttons.

Way 2
Before you attend a general creative writing class, note down the skills you would like to practice and learn. The idea of a student taking responsibility for their own learning process is not widespread, but those who take this proactive step benefit enormously.

13   Entering the world of fiction

The world of fiction from a new writer's perspective

Your first thoughts and responses prepare you to write your own stories with a greater awareness for two key things:

- the fundamental considerations that underpin all fiction
- a writer's relationship with story material.

Informative Overviews on story

In story-writing sessions, the first question I ask students is...

> *What's the most damning thing you can say about a story?*

The answer is 'it's predictable'.

The second question I ask is:

> *'What do you think makes a good story start?'*

Natural Break

Stop reading now and jot down your ideas. This is something that, in practice, few newcomers to story-writing get right on a first attempt. So it needs the time and space that allow the important points to emerge. New writers may understand the concept, but that doesn't guarantee that when putting it into practice, that it will automatically happen.

The reason why this concept-to-practice move is unreliable is because of the need writers have to 'write themselves into' a story. 'Writing yourself into a story' is a good ploy, it is excellent story writing preparation. The fine distinction to make concerns locating and isolating the point the *real* story starts.

The first part of the answer is *'a hook'.*

The second part of the answer is *'a point of rising action'* and/or *'change in the character's life'.*

These two characteristics need to be present and identifiable at the story start.

Story hook

For the writer, hooks become 'pegs to hang a story on'. 'To hook the reader into your story' carries the meaning of landing a fish with lures, temptations and teasers. The hook has to function in both ways, as a peg for your story and a lure for your reader.

Hooks take many forms. Below are three hooks - common story starts.

1   A short dramatic scene of action. Something hap pening that the reader can follow, without fully understanding why it's happening.

2   Dialogue. A character saying something that catches the reader's attention as being interesting or intriguing.

3   An outrageous or unexpected statement that leads directly into the heart of the story.

The third question I ask students is:

In stories written by people new to writing, certain problems recur. One of them is 'the story doesn't fulfil the potential set up at the start'. Why do you think that happens?

To this question, there is no right answer. What happens at this moment is that new writers begin an inner scan, and imagine themselves in the position of being a storywriter who has written a great start. Three possible answers are:

1   The writer got tired.

2   The writer got bored with his material.

3   The writer lost the feeling s/he had at the start of the story and didn't know how to recapture it.

On the surface, these three are good answers.

The deeper answers are:

1   The writer lost faith, stopped trusting the personal fire contained in the original image. Prosaically, inspiration waned.

2   The writer forgot s/he 'had to go further', let the image develop. S/he didn't wrestle with the material.

3   The writer cut off too soon. Forgot to - 'engage with your material'.

4   The writer became focused on the production of words, not meaning.

5   The writer over-focused on the goal – finishing the story, somehow, anyhow.

6   The writer lost – or thought s/he'd lost deep emotional connection to the story.

7   The writer trusted Left Brain.

8   The writer forgot to move forward into the story action.

The practical answer may well be: There's so much to think about, that producing an ending that tops the story-start may never surface in the writer's mind. Unless the ending is considered in isolation and focused on, with the attention to detail that produces a range of possible dénouements. So the story fizzles out rather than deeply satisfies the reader.

A fourth question I ask is:

'Why do you think stories fizzle out?'

It's the same question as the third one of course, expressed slightly differently to refocus attention on plot.

The character-driven plot

The character-driven plot is a concept that contains two main ideas. The first is that what happens to the story-character results from the kind of person s/he is. This is a little restrictive. The more useful and richer framework is that the weaknesses and vulnerabilities of the story-characters are tested through plot. These two interpretations serve the emotionally-based story well, but high-action drama relies on great plotting. The best book on plotting I've read is Ansen Dibell's book *Plot* (Robinson Publishing 1-85487-069-6).

A reader-based understanding of story

What do readers want from a story?

Students often circle around the two main answers to this question, one which addresses the reader's mindstate while reading, the other the overall effect of fiction reading. Why readers read fiction.

The ensuing discussion arising from the question *'What do readers want from a story?'* may range way outside my personal understanding and appreciation, bring up areas which surprise me but may fascinate students so need an airing. Such as *'How far, or in what ways, do stories mirror life?'* or *'In what ways is life your story-model?'* Aslant perceptions are good triggers for story ideas.

These questions take discussions into the area of individual perception and can be revelatory – especially to the writers themselves. But such discussions enlarge the field of play, open up more possibilities, and are expansive in their effect on the mind of the new writer. They may even give them an insight into that fundamental question.

What do readers want most from a story?

1   *To know what happens next.* (Reflecting the reader's mindstate while reading.)

2   *A vicarious experience.* (To live, in imagination, another life, totally different from one's own.)

This process of asking students questions, bringing them back on track, asking more questions, opens up the process of story-making in advance of doing it. It forewarns. But its major job is as a reconnaissance.

A good analogy is: *as when flying over an area to take a look at the land before taking the journey through it yourself, on foot. The questions and answers are like snapshots taken from the air. Guidelines in picture form.*

It also alerts me, as teacher, where students' thinking needs development.

Three traps for new story writers concerning relationship with their story material

Trap 1 – The Real Life Model

In real life, if someone has a problem normally they try to solve it and resolve it in the easiest and simplest way possible. This is the opposite strategy to the one necessary for story-writing, where increasing the pressure on your characters is strongly advised to create tension, pace and page-turning quality.

Enter the new writer. S/he has just created characters s/he loves and put them through – in a story draft – a fair bit of trauma by real life standards. Indeed, the writing of that story may have brought tears – a good sign of emotional connection. Now s/he's asked to find ways to increase the disaster/trauma on these loved characters, in order to make readers identify more strongly with the story. This is where the Real Life Model works against the new writer. S/he will, of course, learn this distinction and be able to rectify matters at the rewrite stage.

Trap 2 – Believing/acting on current feelings/moodstate

It's now believed we create our reality on a moment-by-moment basis. Hence the importance attached to 'living in the now'. All methods serve to power writers through blocks, and turn them into stepping stones. Plant that image firmly in your mind. Just decide stuckness is not an option. Try not to worry. Worry wastes and squanders energy. Just observe. You'll learn about your personal process quicker that way and find what serves you and your writing best.

Trap 3 - Dissociation

Dissociation, in this context, is withdrawal of connection with the story. This usually indicates a need to deepen the story, make it more meaningful to you – and therefore more interesting for your readers. That is, you win and the reader wins.

If this loss of inner fire is interpreted as a sign to cut off, it is wrongly interpreted. Instead, ask yourself 'what would have to happen here to make this story live for me again?' It is one of the most self-supporting and re-energising questions a writer can ask of material that's lost its original fire.

Blocks into stepping stones

Essentially, these three are all emotional traps, presenting themselves in different forms. Label them 'traps' and you give them their real I.D. This will hand you the (metaphorical) trump cards, ways to win over and through their distracting, dissipating and de-energising effects and give you ways to turn blocks into stepping stones. Any self-created metaphor that does that job is (metaphorical) gold to you.

Story and story development, Right Brain style

Story development follows on naturally from imagework in

the sense that it requires a Right Brain approach to get the most out of it.

Interrogation of material as a developmental technique

Interrogation is a tried, tested and trusted way of developing any material or work-in-progress. It operates at the level of re-engagement, a re-arousal of interest in material appearing stale (subjective evaluation) to the writer.

Subjectivity as friend and enemy of the writer

Subjectivity is both friend and enemy to the writer. So far, we've talked a lot about the importance of personalising and individualising in creative work and how this process is fast forwarded by doing imagework which values and brings to your attention this inner knowing. That's where subjectivity works *for* the writer.

There is a danger in subjectivity. If a writer succumbs to the subjective feeling that the work-in-progress has lost power, s/he is no longer interested in it, s/he will miss out on the objective reality. The objective reality is that anything is capable of further development if the passion – willpower – to deepen work is present.

To illustrate this point, look again to J.K. Rowling. Before **Harry Potter,** many other well-published writers explored the subject of witch and wizard schools, and presumably did so to the best of their ability. Some people might consider the subject a 'tired' one long before J.K. Rowling started writing her series.

A more helpful and fruitful line of questioning comes from asking what fundamental difference in attitude distinguishes J.K. Rowling and her 'vision' of witch and wizard schools from these other writers? What quality would you highlight?

1   *Seriousness of commitment – 17 years of her human life to cover the 7 year school experience.*

2   *Seriousness of intent – the good v. evil battle fought throughout teenage years.*

3   *Massive passion for her subject.*

4   A *wonderful imagination that 'goes beyond'. Innovative because it personalises and individualises the story characters and their particular magical abilities and attributes.*

5   *Great sense of humour which never superficialises or trivialises the gravitas, its serious theme. (This is a real danger with fantasy-writing if the 'escapism' element gets over emphasised.)*

6   *No shrinking or avoiding of the reality of life. Magic is used to forward the selfish, cruel and evil agendas of characters far more powerful than the hero. (A great empathy-point between Harry and any child reading the books.)*

7   *Hero tested to the limits and beyond.*

It's obviously a mix of these seven, and no doubt the books' hooking qualities for child-readers could easily top a hundred. But addressing this question helps to make it clear what qualities we need to develop in ourselves as writers. Importantly, it faces us with questions concerning personal passion and our own writing ambitions.

So subjectivity as the enemy is located in dis-engagement from, and loss of interest in, a project which started with enthusiasm and inspiration. (To phrase it like that encourages a dissociation). Go with that subjective feeling and you may well stop writing. People do.

It's a fine line, of course, with factors like tiredness and overwork dulling perceptions and influencing how we feel at any one time.

What are needed are fresh approaches to reawaken the writer's interest. So s/he moves, psychologically, into a higher gear and takes the work to another – more meaningful and significant - level.

There are strategies to overcome this experience of writers' disengagement with their work. New writers are advised to – using a Right Brain analogy - to 'wrestle with their material', and 'become like a dog with a bone'. i.e. refuse to let go till the material yields its potential.

'Wrestling with material' is, of course, a kinaesthetic image which, if taken literally, can be seen as not very productive.

Writer Tip

Anything we think about grows, and it grows particularly well if we apply Right Brain creativity to its nurture. This helps bypass any subjective unhelpful feelings we may have at any time about our relationship to the project in hand.

The transformation of subjective 'don't want to know' to 'raring to go at it again' feeling-states lies in the writer's hands, thoughts and ways s/he deals with it. Remember, to seed this transformation for yourself, the image of 'blocks into stepping stones' is the way to re-frame it.

At the level of the brain, Albert Einstein said all he did that was different to what anyone else did was to 'stay longer with a problem'. So if wrestling with material and dogs doesn't raise personal energies, try aligning your thinking with the humility of a person like Einstein who made amazing scientific breakthroughs.

I've met the problem of dis-engagement with longer projects many times and in many different personalities and it is possible to identify patterns of reasoning which are unhelpful to a writer.

In workshops, we have sessions where I ask people what their biggest problem is, as a writer, and I often hear it's 'the inability to finish things'. It can become a bad habit. It's the feeling behind it all the inspiration-junkie seeks, not a finished piece of work. The priority-list needs attention. Words like goals, motivation and commitment appear, and they are issues every writer faces. Inspiration may take you on a high from beginning to end of a project, but to abandon the project because inspiration is (temporarily) absent is not a good strategy.

The good strategy is to get out the back-up kit. Here, that back-up kit is Right Brain Interrogation of Image. There are times when we need to take charge and Interrogation of Image – marks the changeover, (See Chapter 15). I read the situation of dis-engagement as the one where I can be most useful to students, because a great deal of personal empowerment comes with learning how to go through your own writing blocks. So I almost welcome its appearance because I've witnessed the real and significant power for students of the various Right Brain techniques of interrogation many, many times.

There is a hierarchy within problem-solving for writers which naturally leads to learning.

Expanding the strategy-base for development

First we do the obvious. i.e. Either wait for inspiration or ask Left Brain questions.

Second, we learn alternative methods so our strategy-base increases. We have recourse to a wider field of options and so feel more confident.

Third, we frame the problem differently in the future.

Nevertheless, a block feels like a block, even to the experienced writer.

Consider the following four-point turnaround system.

The 4-point turnaround system

1 Let imagination lead the way. It's energy-full, and is the greatest source of personal creativity anyone possesses. Honour everything about it: how it makes you feel, the wonderful work it produces, how it touches the 'anything's possible' button.

2 Use imagework to re-engage your Right Brain. You know a lot about that now and hopefully have begun to personally experience imagework's power to validate; underpin, reinforce and concretise - as well as draw out - the fullness of your creative ideas

3 Use Action Images, the subject of Chapter 14.

4 Use Interrogation of Image - Chapter 15 - to get you back on track and inspired again.

Something to visualise
Background on visualisation

For fiction, a writer needs drama, tension, excitement, larger than life characters, unpredictable non-linear plot development and high stakes. These patterns, and the imagery that produces them need to be learnt. An automatic translation of the seen or read to the writing rarely happens because the mind mode is different; passive for reading and active for writing. Generally, people read for enjoyment, entertainment and information, not for the structure, techniques and understanding how the writer did it. If the translation from reading to writing does happen, it is often derivative. A proof of this is when publishers report a flood of submissions of a certain type of story in the wake of a best-selling success.

One way to kick-start the process of learning new thinking patterns is to cultivate the facility to think 'outside the box'. Thinking outside the box, even for a few minutes as a fun exercise, provides a precious newness from which great ideas can spring.

Brainstorming, as we know, values the most bizarre idea as the one which is ultimately likely to offer a breakthrough to a problem. This goes against logic and common sense. Logic and common sense have their place here too, but they need to be applied to the bizarre idea at Stage 2 of the process, not Stage 1. In this, we once again see the pattern of the Left Brain decoding, interpreting, making possible the Right Brain's creative offerings, to form the best creative partnership between the two brain hemispheres.

An easy way to teach our brains new patterns is to go outside the area of study, - here it is creative writing, - and draw on perceptions from other specialisms. Here, we'll use garden design as our template. The modern show garden reflects how gardeners are becoming more design conscious and finding ways to interpret their concepts into 3-D gardens to delight the public.

The visualisation - Fantasy garden

Imagine your perfect garden. Get as much detail and colour as you can. This is not an exercise in learning Latin names for plants or the kind of micro climates they require to flourish. You need no gardening skills at all, just your imagination to create a space which you'd love and enjoy to the utmost. It is a fantasy garden and, as such, it's a no holds barred situation. You are not creating this garden to take to Chelsea, but to give you insights into preferences, loves, interests, what delights your eye and full sensual awareness. On this point, you might like to remind yourself of the extended visualisation you did in Chapter 8. Gardens are one place where people are encouraged to indulge and develop their senses of smell, touch, taste and sound.

In your Learning Journal, record as much of the concrete detail as you can, as you would a dream.

Ways into fiction
Way 1

In your Learning Journal record what you have learnt from the Q. & A. sections of this chapter. After you've recorded it, explore it in your own language and style. Say in what ways you think this wider understanding will help you in the future as a writer. Bring it back to the personal empowering level.

Way 2

Check out story starts for yourself. Any story you happen to read or have read. Become story hook-happy. Develop your awareness of the underlying techniques used in the story hook. Feel how it works, pulls you into a story. It's that same feeling-level you want to recapture with your own story starts. Go one stage further and compare story starts. Which ones are particularly powerful for you and why? Answering that will take you deeper into your own creative process and prepare you for story writing.

14 Story Writing – Way 1

Writers use many methods to improve their story writing technique. The more 'handles' you have on story technique, the firmer and stronger your grasp of essentials. This translates as *diverse* approaches to the same task, a rich contextualisation – with the aim of writing a great story that satisfies both you and the reader. Visualise it as an all-round-approach.

In this chapter we will consider four complementary approaches:

- you already know, at the intuitive level, what makes a good story.
- an iceberg as an appropriate metaphor for the process of story creation.
- focused reading of stories to deeply understand structure and weave.
- role playing your fictional characters

Intuitive wisdom concerning story

Even if you have never yet written a story, you already know what a good story is. This is because, as a culture, we are exposed from infancy to story in many different forms – the written word, play, dvd, film.

You can have great fun by asking 'what makes a story great, for you?'

By this route, students move forward into the kind of stories they'd personally like to write. What you deeply admire it's natural to emulate. In terms of creativity, draw on it as inspiration to power you into your individual way of relating to and expressing that admired quality. This adds up to a complete reinvention, your style.

At the intuitive-feeling state, it's absolutely true that a new writer already knows what a good story is. In the western world, we are brought up on a diet of stories. Throughout our education, we have masses of exposure to the experience of reading stories (what happens next) and the end product (the vicarious satisfaction of living another life entirely different to our own).

> **Writer Tip**
>
> If you disagree with this simplistic overview, note down in your Learning Journal why and also what you consider the most important aspect or aspects of good story. My personal learning curve always rocketed at the moment I realised that I fundamentally disagreed with the perception of a teacher, facilitator or writer. Over time, I discovered that to follow my own line was vital and key to developing both my ideas and the direction of my writing.

Some people, even today, relate to other people mainly through a story-telling rather than fact-giving mindset. It's natural to them.

Here, we are still talking in overviews, remember. Still holding to the big picture mindstate, the *wholism** which is a Right Brain function.

Creative writing teachers and speakers on writing tend to emphasise certain points about story writing, e.g. the chaotic and unpredictable nature of creative process, being 'taken over' by story characters, the 'getting lost' in the writing. This is done to prepare novice writers for what they will meet and experience if they take up writing as hobby or profession. It's delivered Left Brain (verbal) with the intention of calling up the Right Brain state in new writers. I've yet to see anyone produce a picture, though sometimes speakers produce their picture-*file*. A store of characters they use as physical models - photographic lookalikes - for their story characters.

Using Right Brain storymaking methods will not guarantee you write a publishable story first time. This is because there are too many mini-skills that have to be brought together seamlessly in the finished story, and this requires a facility with certain ways of thinking which need grooving in.

The different levels a new writer has to integrate and synthesise is an entirely new skill. It isn't that it's *difficult*, it's that *different organisational frameworks* are needed. (This is where N.L.P. practitioners are at an advantage, because they are used to putting different frameworks on ideas, pictures, mental material, mindstuff.)

This background information is important to know because new writers tend to become impatient with themselves when, in actuality, they are in a state of over-expectation. They've seen nothing but finished stories. Simple, clear, focused, gripping tales.

Storymaking as an iceberg-metaphor

With icebergs, all you see is that iceberg tip. Supporting it, underwater, out of sight, is another nine-tenths of iceberg. All the public sees of a writer's work is the published story; that other nine-tenths of the work that went into it is out of sight and rarely considered unless the writer is interviewed by the media.

A lot of headwork – mental organising and reorganising is needed to tweak a first draft into a finished story. For beginners, the process of development and the first draft often get muddled up. Even professional writers often have to 'write themselves into' a story. The main difference here is the more experienced writer will be quicker to pick up where the story starts – the point of rising action when the character faces change, challenge or trauma. This facility, this sensitivity to the right place to start a story, happens because they've been through the story-creating process many times before. So there is an awareness – a constant scan in the back of their minds for this moment of 'rising action'. They know it signals the story start.

Problems with new writers' stories

Typically, new writers' stories have three problems. As with the three traps concerning the relationship the writer has with story making generally.

1   Predictability

There's a very good reason why newcomers write predictable stories. For the new writer, his or her story will not feel predictable. S/he is in a *reinventing-the-wheel* simply because s/he's never written a story before, or not since schooldays. So, for the writer, it's a first time experience. For the reader, it's the 'same old experience'. The two are worlds apart.

2 Telling & static writing

The 'what happens next?' gets lost in getting one to two thousand words onto the page. New writers have to develop an aversion for stasis, those times when the story stops because the writer is explaining something. (Telling, not showing.) This is a *planning* job, and will need a backtrack to sort it. It's addressed and refocused in an enabling way by *reframing* the story, and answering one simple question. 'What scenes will best *show* my story?'

Another way of saying this is the Left Brain temporarily gets the upper hand in the striving for a logical (Left Brain) story development. The 'show, don't tell' advice is lost. Pictures and scenes desert the new writer's mind because s/he is just too Left Brain in orientation in an effort to sort out the logistics.

3 The vicarious satisfaction for the reader doesn't come through because the new writer has yet to learn that complete identification with story characters. The one which leads some professional writers to exclaim 'I know my story-characters better than my friends and relatives!'

The Right Brain link is to role-playing: to become the story-character, answer questions as the story-character, much as an actor does in preparation for performance.

Ways into story

The easiest way into story is to look at one, and put different frameworks on it. This gives you a feeling for the story-weave, and how you can tease it apart. Extract one aspect and examine it close up. A much loved fairy tale is as good as a modern commercial short story because they both offer the same the chance to look at the story-weave.

It's also an exercise in focusing.

The interactive reading of story

We can read with any agenda. The first important distinction is the reader/writer. We can read as does a reader – for enjoyment, information, a mind-distraction. We can read as a *writer* – to see what other writers do. Generally, it's a good idea to read as a reader first and then to reread with a variety of foci.

Here are four useful interactive ways to read a story and *engage* with it to enhance your awareness of its major elements and their integration.

1   Read for plot
2   Read for emotion
3   Read for character and character development
4   Read for mind-pictures

Way 1 – Read for plot

Isolate the action. Be disciplined about this because it pays great dividends. In 10 or 12 sentences maximum, extract the line of action from your chosen story. You will find the first couple of sentences are easy enough. As the action of the story becomes more complicated, you will have to reconsider, re-phrase, redo, some of your sentences to fit it into the sentence limit. This is great practice at rewriting, a primer in reordering a basic sentence to achieve clarity and get your main points across.

For the plot-shy writer – and there are many   it demonstrates how action is intensified. It builds an awareness in new writers that was often not previously present. This awareness can then be carried over into your own strategy-base for story-writing.

Though it's only a 10 sentence exercise, it is quite hard work if you are not used to thinking in terms of plot. Take the level of difficulty you experience doing this exercise as an indicator of your plot-happy or unhappy status! If it's hard to do, practice on another story. You really do need this skill if you want to write fiction.

Way 2 – Read for emotion

Record the emotions – the *succession* of emotions - you feel on reading the story. Or, if the story is too familiar, record the emotions you believe the writer wanted to create in the reader. If it's just one emotion, record its strength on a 1–10 scale, where 1 is not much, and 10 is full emotion.

This writer/reader interface gives you many handles on the subtext of a story. This is the place of vicarious experience. Never forget readers read for emotion. For the emotions they feel through imagining themselves living through the experiences encountered by the story hero or heroine.

Way 3 – Read for character and character development

Find a way to relate to the main character. Remember, relational rather than analytical is the way to keep it a Right Brain function. To think of the character's journey through the story can help to give the distance and perspective necessary to see this clearly. Look closely at the beginning and end of the story and spend some time considering how and why the main character has changed in the course of the story. Be definite about it. *'At the start of the story the main character was... At the end s/he was... The reason/s s/he changed (or grew) was because...'*

By doing this exercise you are in-building in yourself an awareness and sensitivity to another important requirement of story... That is, how the main character changes, learns, grows, as a result of what happens to him or her in the story. The particular weave of a story – the character-plot bond – becomes more visible to you through this deeper looking at the character's personality and motivations.

Way 4 – Read for mind-pictures

Often I ask new students to do just one thing while I read a story. Close their eyes and become aware of the inner images - *scenes* - they get while the story is being read. A development of this is to write the strongest mind-picture out in detail, adding their personal embellishments. Things they 'see' in their mind picture but which aren't actually there in the story-scene. To read for mind-pictures (scenes) is a wonderful demonstration of the unspoken writer/reader contract – the Right Brain/ Right Brain communication set up through story imagery.

Natural break

Close your eyes now and see which image from your chosen story comes most alive for you. Record this scene in detail, adding little touches of your own, things not in the original scene from this story at all. It's a proactive creative move, and seems to break the thrall that can stop writers from making imaginative leaps. As usual, the advice is to be bold.

Role-play your characters

Look. There's no-one watching. You don't need to feel self-conscious about interrogating the characters you've created. Or, more accurately, are in the process of creating. To be precise, you, as story-writer, have a dialogue outloud with you, as story-character.

To write from inside a character, you have to get to know them better, and the best way to do that is to spend lots of time with them. Even take them into situations outside the story-one, and see how they behave then. This is exactly the method used in the famous play *'Abigail's Party'* where the actors interacted with each other for several days *in character*. At this first stage, the actors did it without knowing the situation they were going to have to deal with and resolve in the play itself. Initially the actors energies were focused on discovering and understanding the character they were playing and their relationships with all the other characters. At the time, it was a novel way of writing a play – a wholly organic process that had a preparatory phase of living the life of someone else.

In a writing workshop, the story-writer 'becomes' the character for the duration of an exercise where the rest of the group ask questions of him or her. This *hot seat* treatment dis allows the 'I don't know' reply. If you *are* the character, you invent, on the spot, a fictional history. Students quake a bit at the start but, by the end of the session they have learned so much about their characters they recognise the power of the exercise. It literally *powers them through* to a new appreciation of the characters they are creating.

Four direct benefits of role-playing your characters

1   You are using a Right Brain method. All you have to do is work through that self-conscious stage. A character-happy writer is one who enjoys making characters spring to life in this

interactive way.

2   You are practising dialogue creation. A modern story consists of 60% dialogue, so you are practising a valuable skill.

3   You will discover more about your characters. They will feel more real and alive to you, so you will be less inclined to move them about as if they were puppets of the action.

4   Ultimately, you will write a better story through doing this depth-work with your characters.

Do not be put off by the fact the first questions you ask your character feels superficial or 'silly'. Go through it. It won't last long.

The signal you are on the right track is when you run out of 'obvious' questions and start to ask 'meaningful' (meaningful to you) ones. It's at the point of *engagement* with your story material and story characters that the process moves to another level where your story idea takes fire and reveals more of its potential.

Something to visualise
Animation and Anthropomorphism

A good startpoint is to look at how animation and anthropomorphism are tagged and viewed in western culture. That is, consider their public image. Think about it for a moment.

Mainly for children, particularly younger children and with an inherited tendency to be considered as twee, talking animals. Fringe, marginal, not serious.

(I hope you are hotly disagreeing here!)

The *effect* of this demotion of animation and anthropomorphism as a literary form on new writers is erosive. A cut-off, a don't go there, *don't do fantasy, realism's more important,* kind of take.

The end result on students is often even more interesting. It can include an unwillingness to experiment, an increase in self-consciousness within the writing, a backing-off rather than diving into inherent potential. A cultural block comes into play.

Let's reframe animation and anthropomorphism to up its credibility.

1   It is yet another form of imagination-stretch.   It should be classified that way, given equal status to any other imagination-stretch exercise.

2   Adopt the Models Approach. This is the approach that turns the perceptions so far outlined on their head. The aim of the BBC's Big Read 2004 Competition was to find the nation's all-time favourite reads, the best fiction ever written according to a modern audience.

Four out of the five winners were fantasy books. J.R.R. Tolkien's *The Lord of the Rings* came first; Philip Pullman's *His Dark Materials* third, Douglas Adams *Hitchhiker's Guide to the Galaxy* fourth, and J.K. Rowling's *Harry Potter and the Goblet of Fire* fifth.

We'll start with the winner, J.R.R. Tolkien's *The Lord of the Rings*. For the purpose of this exercise, we'll focus on the Ents.   Ents are walking talking trees who fight, with a history that gives them plenty of emotional baggage and character.

The visualisation - anthropomorphising

Metaphorically, take a leaf out of J.R.R. Tolkien's book. As fully as you can, visualise an anthropomorphised tree or plant. Does it speak? Perhaps, like J.K. Rowling's womping willow that hits everything that approaches it, it relies on actions to speak louder than words.

In your Learning Journal, record what age-group of reader you feel your anthropomorphised tree or plant would suit. Once that distinction is made and in place, its fit in a literary sense is easier to imagine.

Way into Character

A spontaneous character-invention exercise

Off the top of your head, invent a character. Jot down the absolute basics: Name, age, occupation, marital status, current problem. Imagine meeting with this character in a specific setting, - cafe, park, on a hill, by a river, in a wood. So it feels grounded and real to you. Imagine you already know this person, so this is a meeting with an old acquaintance you haven't seen for a long time. It's also a signal to your subconscious mind that you know far more about this character than you first thought you did.

So you can leap – imaginatively – straight into the relationship. Because there'll be quite a lot of catching up to do.

To get a good level, and not superficial chit-chat, ask practical questions about the current life situation (which will lead naturally to plot-related) together with ones that are more intimate.

Here's a few questions to give you a start. You'll need to give them a context.

1   I thought you said you'd never do that? What changed your mind?
2   What are you doing now?
3   When do you plan to start?
4   What happened afterwards?
5   What's the thing you most dread?
6   What would you most like to happen?

Story Writing – Way 2

Action Images as fiction's source

Way 2 into story writing directly tackles the two big recurring problems with new writers' stories. These are:

1   Predictability – in development and/or denouement
2   'Telling' a story, instead of 'showing' a story.

Action Images address both these problems directly. The writer is sourcing story material in Right Brain moving image and this has amazing effects on how s/he organises and subsequently processes story material. This method can be seen as quite as effective as the strategy of 'cutting out the middleman' in the commercial world. Only here what is getting 'cut out' is the unnecessary and unwanted 'telling'. 'Telling' doesn't get a look-in. It's factored out completely. Instead, the writer's mind is focused on the translation of moving image-in-mind to the same on page. Action. And Image.

What is an Action Image?

An Action Image is an image where something is happening. It really is that simple. To continue the use of a metaphorical language, an Action Image is like a film or video shot, rather than a photo or a static visualisation of an object or event.

Action Images and imagework

The imagework journey in this book started with inner image as mind-replays of familiar scenes and moved on to high visualisation exercises designed to deliberately conjure hundreds of images and reach the Image-happy state. Then, by using metaphor, we explored the aligning of personal meaning to pictures in two major contexts – the corpus callosum and the 'Life is...' metaphor. With Action Images, the writer enters the world of fiction and fictional development, the subject of this chapter.

Action Images and writers

A professional writer can happily work off a single Action Image but beginners need more – two to four Action Images - to kickstart the fictional development process.

Creating or coming up with a variety of Actions Images is not about a learnt skill, in the sense of being something exterior and outside the writer. Its source is the same one we have been drawing on (as in using and bringing to the front of awareness) throughout this book. It's belief and reliance on inner imagery.

Inner imagery as universal currency

The American writer, Jean Houston, author of *The Mythic Life* (HarperSanFrancisco 0-06-250281-6) has worked with inner imagery and its power, with peoples across the world. She and her partner have isolated the same factors in operation with respect to inner imagery, regardless of race, background, education and experience. Jean says:

'Inner imagery taps into domains of the self that are available all the time, and which offer vast reservoirs of unconscious knowledge to the creative process. The further into these domains one goes, the richer the solutions will be.... We are storied and storying beings to our core.'

Why it's important to know the power of deep imagery work

Deep imagery work is part of many modern psychotherapies. For people generally, it offers easy and immediate access to self-knowledge. If you have done the exercises so far through 'Ways Into Image' you will already be aware of this aspect. As writers, we use inner imagery for a different but related purpose, - to access the personally meaningful for story material.

Earlier we talked of the double filters that keep many people out of touch with reliance, deep reliance, on inner knowing through imagework. The first is the culture which keeps people outer-focused; on the latest, the upcoming or fashionable. The second is our Left Brain biased training, which undermines and undervalues Right Brain functioning. Most of us buy into this double filter without questioning it, because it is powerful and persuasive, especially *logically* persuasive.

In *The Mythic Life* Jean Houston reveals that, by working with and changing inner imagery (to something carrying empowering and positive rather than negative connotations) deep cultural patterns that keep a people in habitually victimised and depowered mindstates can be shifted. Change at a *cultural* level is no easy matter. To discover it is at the level of *imagery* that breakthrough is possible is an exciting and illuminating demonstration of Right Brain power.

If inner imagery works so powerfully at the cultural level, then perhaps writers should approach personal imagery for storymaking with deep respect.

Jean Houston's work with cultures worldwide is important background knowledge to our working with Action Images today. It doesn't stop new writers producing crazy, hilarious and utterly weird Action Images, and nor should it! The major effect of knowing this background to inner imagery gleaned from advances in psychotherapy is it gives writers a fuller understanding of imagework's potential. It's then up to the individual writer to choose a line of approach that appeals and will best serve his or her writing or current writing need, aspiration or ambition.

The goal here is to become Action Image happy. Then learn to use those Action Images to produce stories stamped with individuality and uniqueness coupled to a *universality* that makes them memorable to yourself, editors and readers.

Approaches to Action Images

It's a natural progression to move from image-making to Action Images, from the static to the dynamic. If 'what is going on in the image' is also in some way mysterious it becomes an ideal start-point for a fictional piece. That is story, poem or play. The Action Image can therefore be seen as a fast-track, possessing the all-in-one quality which takes the writer into story potential at the first step.

Reading, interpreting and using Action Images in fiction

By now, we know a number of things about images generally. These understandings help and inform us as we start to work with them.

1   The first one, as always with this book, is the reassurance of knowing we are sourcing our work in the Right Brain. By using the Right Brain language of image-speak, we automatically call up a full range of imaginative skills.

2   Personal image interpretation is just that. We all see different things in images, read into them our own meanings.

3   With the addition of fictional development, a new factor comes into play. It's vital to remember that a picture or image gives us a surface appearance. That surface appearance may be deceptive, may not reflect what's really going on in the story. It may have a 'red herring' quality. Translated into image-reading, this means that:

A totally bizarre image can have a rational explanation. A mundane scene can hide a wealth of amazing facts.

Writer Tip

These reframings of what is happening in an image, or what might be happening and how it relates to the overall story are important. They teach you to remain flexible, not fix a definite meaning too quickly, to stay open-minded. This is a mindset a writer needs to cultivate, hone, rely on, court, and learn to deeply trust. In this lies the essence of creativity. More prosaically, writers learn to accept that the first or tenth idea may not the best. What may finally be used is Idea Number 9 combined with a bit of Idea 3 and draw off the mindset that originally seeded Idea Number 7.

Randomness, remember, is a Right Brain quality and needs to be worked with, not against. And certainly not despaired over! Keeping an open mind is the *only* effective way to work with that random quality.

As stated earlier, if you are new to this way of working, it's better to use several Action Images for your story... This keys into a basic rule of creativity.

Golden Guideline

Creativity happens when two things are brought together that have never been brought together previously. This applies to specific subjects, ideas, to people, their relationships, ideas and of course, to Action Images.

This background opens up and sets up the inherent potential for working with Action Images in this way. It gives the rational which allows us to immediately see its power and strength at the creative level.

The problem here is not students' resistance to doing the exercise itself. It's their attitude which is coloured by a tendency to have a closed mindset and cut off too early.

The reasons this happens is because:

1   On the surface, all they're working with are several unrelated pictures or images

2   They are new to the method, so have little reason to trust it implicitly.

3   Students don't have the one big advantage you have, as reader. In this book so far you've done vastly more imagework than does an average student on a writing course. You are already an image-happy and metaphor-happy writer. So you are in the empowered position to naturally override points 1 and 2.

Fifty Action Images

These Action Images were worked up by my partner and myself. As such, they reflect our interests and concerns. When reading them, remember the advice to 'look beneath surface appearances' as a first move into meaning, into decoding 'what's going on here?' or 'what *might* be going on here?'

1   A mynah bird sitting on a post makes rude remarks at passers-by.

2   Paper boy walking across waste ground.

3   Flowers move on a pond but there is no wind.

4   Troupe of uniformed gibbons greets Head of State at Third World airport.

5   One legged man hurls crutch at vicar during sermon.

6   Scientist enters conference. He announces 'there's great advantages to holes in the ozone layer'.

7   Three masked men raid a bank. One demands a million pounds. The other two throw popcorn at staff and customers.

8   Boy flying kite sees a butterfly mimicking the kite's movements.

9   Overnight, a crater appears in a field. Magnetic repulsion stops people getting near it.

10   Photo taken at monastery reveals monks who were not there when the photo was taken.

11   Two black unlicensed cares hurtle down a country lane. One contains four nuns, the other four generals.

12   An escaped kangaroo develops an attraction for cats and kittens which follow him.

13   The Maharishi bestows blessings on his people each day. But today he appears with a black eye and a limp.

14   A dolphin, programmed for war, holes boats in a local harbour.

15   As the sun comes up in Agra, the Taj Mahal has disappeared. Next day it reappears, and the Black Taj Mahal on the other side of the river stands resplendent.

16   Lady Emily Foley presents prizes at a Flower Show in 1857. The huge winning cucumber flies out of the window.

17   Car travelling at speed on motorway loses wheel. Driver sees wheel overtake him.

18   Farmer discovers a knight in armour digging up his potatoes.

19   At an animal sanctuary, a demented rabbit gets onto a roof, dislodges tiles, which then fall on two cats, killing them.

20   Hedgehog climbs over wall. Slips and falls on a couple making love, prickling them.

21   A stone is thrown through a window with a message attached which doesn't make sense.

22   Leader in a marathon enters Stadium. He's attacked and stripped by three women in white robes.

23   Police stop a speeding car. Driver is a monk under a vow of silence. Passenger speaks only Yiddish.

24   Light aircraft makes emergency landing in a field. Farmer, harvesting, continues to cut the corn, leaving shape of plane in field.

25   Whitehall. Queen gets a bunch of roses in her lap, laser bombed from a Phantom jet in a fly past.

26   Camel taught to move his lips as though speaking, for advertising purposes.

27   Two climbers reach top of previously unclimbed Himalayan peak. They meet one man in white robes and a horned creature with a forked tail, cloven hooves, carrying a trident.

28   Village church service conducted by a large green man, speaking an incomprehensible language.

29   During church service, the Reverend Soames finds water turned into wine.

30   A conversation between a crow pecking the ground and an earthworm who emerges.

31   On a housing estate, the ice cream man and the milkman rolls up their sleeves for a punch up. Their white coats are held by children.

32   Ascot. Ladies Day. As the landaus drive along the course, there is an explosion.

33   Police arrest a naked jogger. He tells them he is God.

34   A herdsman looks up. He sees four flying yogis on mat. A fifth mat carries a tiger in the lotus position.

35   A hearse pursued by the police, doing eighty down the motorway, flowers flying off its roof.

36   Wembley Stadium. Cup Final day. As the crowd sings 'Abide with me' the Stadium lifts off the Earth into the sky.

37   An English park with rhododendrons. A band plays. A bear emerges from the rhododendrons, snatches a bandsman and goes back into the shrubbery.

38   Astronauts return from space. What they had two of before, they now have four. What they had one of, they now have two.

39   Presidential motorcade joined by a car containing four orang-utans.

40   Because of pressure on land, an animal hybrid is produced which is rideable, milkable and produces wool.

41   Cape Canaveral. Five minutes before lift-off, the Feds turn up with an arrest warrant for two astronauts in the capsule.

42   Flying animal turns itself into a boomerang shape so it can come back effortlessly.

43   Planning consent so difficult, a worm needs one for a wormcast, a mole for a molehill.

44   Anti-violence image. Hit something, it gets bigger. Kill it, it returns twenty times larger.

45   Two U.S. Navy pilots, launched on an air strike, can't hear instructions and have to abort because of music in their headphones playing 'Oh I do like to be beside the seaside'.

46   Church bell sounding on one note changes to cheerful ditty.

47   A sheep, begging food off tourists, climbs into a woman's car. She pulls wool off it.

48   A yak, brought down to sea level, is given 'mountain air' in a mask, so it can survive at this lower altitude.

49   As a result of a Virtual Reality experience, a person's normal filters break down.

50   Motorway traffic brought to a standstill by an army of hedgehogs marching backwards and forwards across the carriageways.

Something to visualise
Background on visualisation

This last visualisation is sourced three ways.

1   The literary link is with Philip Pullman's *His Dark Materials*, the fantasy novel that won 3rd prize in the BBC 2004 Big Read Competition. We are borrowing and reinventing Pullman's concept of daemons. Daemons are creatures who sit on the shoulders of both adults and child, fixed in adult form, shape-changing in children.

2   The animal-helper, a familiar character in children's stories.

3   An extraordinarily successful Confidence Workshop I ran at Swanwick Writers Summer School that used this daemon/animal helper as central character. I say extraordinarily successful because a career-change or lifestyle change that results from a one or two-hour workshop is astonishing.

Not everyone likes animals but we all possess what is termed an animal nature. Do not let your fondness or otherwise for animals influence you here for this is a great exercise in self-empowerment as well as being an imagination-stretch and a chance to role-play a fictional character. Again, take the visualisation at the level personally useful.

The Visualisation - Animal helper
Allow yourself the luxury of imagining a shoulder-mate, whether in the form of an animal-helper, a daemon, or a creature of pure fantasy. Visualise this shoulder-mate as clearly, strongly and colourfully as you can. Take a look at its eyes. Now ask your shoulder-mate for advice concerning your writing. Next, ask your shoulder-mate to share with you the one thing it'll whisper in your ear at moments in the future when you need a little help.

Record in your Learning Journal what your shoulder-mate said. What's the advice with regard to your writing? What did s/he tell you that you didn't already know? How has your thinking and understanding developed?

This visualisation is powerful. You might like to draw your shoulder-mate, for the additional understandings that emerge from concretising the imaginal. A year after doing this workshop, students report their daemons are still on their office walls, providing ongoing support.

Ways into Action Images
Choose a way into Action Images that either appeals, or will serve your current writing needs. Or, just for a change, choose what you feel will be 'difficult to do'. You may be pleasantly surprised!

1   The Interactive Way
Choose ten out of the fifty Action Images given in this chapter. Add one thing to each, to personalise it. This serves as practice at an important writer skill, that of taking anything and making it yours, ensuring it works for you. It's a useful mindset for a writer to develop and hone. It also seeds an ease, facility and confidence to 'take anything' and reinvent or change it to suit your fictional purpose.

2   Invent your own Action Images
From cold, invent as many Action Images as you can. Fifty is

good, but don't stop before twenty-five. You need to learn and experience that feeling of 'pushing' and then see how it rewards you. In your Learning Journal, record how easy or difficult this process is. Does it get easier after you've come up with ten Action Images? This is about Mastery Learning. That is, learning the skill which will allow you to use it and apply it in lots of future writing situations where development is paramount.

3   Action Images as a refresh to story development

To do this, you need to have a story you're working on and would like to develop further. Invent fifty Action Images which use the characters of your story but have no relationship to the current action or storyline. Yes, fifty. It's necessary to do the sort of blitzing of material that fifty images produces to get through your habitual thinking about the story. It's great Right Brain practice for teaching you to 'go way outside your normal parameters'. It will feel like work, pushing your material in this way but it aligns rather well with the old adage about writing being '10% inspiration and 90% perspiration'. The bonus of using Action Images in this way is it moves a tired story onto another level, and shows you fifty ways to dimensionalise without you getting too deeply into any of them. So you are in the more empowered position to stand back and have a good look at a nice range of options. The bonus is that doing this fifty-image once changes your thinking-frames. It's a paradigmshift for the mind. Next time you are in a similar position, you know the route through, out of it, and forwards.

16 The Art of Creative Technique

Fictional Development using Action Images

One thing that must be emphasised with regard to fictional development is that there are no rules other than the open mind, flexibility of approach and the importance of following your own intuition. Nevertheless, you create an expanded base for choice by 'thinking outside the box'.

This means any combination of the following:
- putting a smallish idea into a largish setting.
- making the personal, universal. So it relates to us all, and we relate to it.
- substituting massive repercussions for a story-event originally conceived as just having a small downside.

In whatever ways come to hand, heart and head, the effect of using any of these is to increase the significance of basic story material. This significance usually translates as making a story more dramatic and/or emotionally stronger. These are the areas where beginner writers often fail to develop the potential in their material. To put it colloquially, they don't think 'big' enough. 'Bigging up' ideas is something all writers have to train their minds to do – automatically. After a while, it becomes so automatic to do it, the writer may not even be conscious of this deep patterning concerning the way s/he processes story material.

It all begins when the new writer learns the phrase 'What if..?', starts to use it, and discovers s/he's struck (metaphorical) gold. 'What if' opens the mind to the range of possibilities contained within the divergent / random / non-linear / infinitive developmental approaches which are all Right Brain functions underneath that image/ imaginative / subjective complex.

Following your intuition

To follow your own intuition will take you into ways of working with your story material and chosen Action Images that will surprise. It may even take you away from the precision of the model given in the upcoming example. This is quite O.K., and perfectly normal because of that *divergent* quality of Right Brain processing. It's to be welcomed, rather than worried over. New writers who have yet to develop a deep belief in their own intuition may baulk at the *inexactness* of giving creativity its freedom to that extent. Remember, to pull up and point up 'inexactness' in working method, process or fictional development is Left Brain speak and will not serve story creativity in any way.

The model of working given in the following example is just that, a model.

Creating a storyline from your own Action Images

Read through the rest of this chapter with the intention of using it as a model for creating your own storyline from four Action Images. If this sounds prescriptive, don't worry, it isn't. What is seeded and suggested here is a method of thinking and working with story material that is expansive in nature, so accesses and reveals inherent potential.

Parameters for working with Action Images are...

1 Choose two to four of your Action Images.

2 You can change one thing about two of your Action Images. Adapt them to suit the developing storyline.

3 Interrogate them individually with no intention of joining them up. Joining them up is the big temptation. Many new writers do it, even when asked not to! They cannot resist the impulse to get them all together a.s.a.p. Especially if the 'obvious link' stares them in the face. Avoid the obvious link. That's far too Left Brain. That's your predictable plot. That's no good.

Instead, try holding them apart as long as you possibly can. (Again, this is an opposite move to the natural one. At the writer-level, it's like the earlier example of the writer extricating characters too soon from their problems because s/he loves them, rather than turning the screws on them to serve the plot and story strength.) It's jumping the gun, rather than enriching the story-weave. If you feel an immediate connection in your Action Images coming on, delete it, zap it. Don't let it take hold in your mind. The single big problem that occurs time and again with this exercise and weakens its effectiveness is 'joining up the Action Images too soon'. Joining them up is Stage 2. Interrogating them individually is Stage 1.

This is one of a couple of problems that occur with this exercise. They both act as 'warnings to the writer'. Warnings that a strategy-change is needed in order to get the best out of their material.

The second problem, of course, is its opposite. A total inability to connect two, three or four Action Images. The remedy here is to invent a Link Image. Something not yet introduced, like a Wild Card, that is the connector between three or four images.

At this point, 'wrestling with your material' may start to take on an unexpected reality. Try and reframe this experience as laying down a working foundation for fiction creation and writing which will serve you for a lifetime. To think of it that way is healthier, easier on the mind, and also true.

'Bigging up' Working Titles

Give the storyline you are about to create a working title. Again it's something students often avoid, because it involves a real mental push to find one. Yet Working Titles are unbelievably helpful to writers. Here's five jobs Working Titles do. Working titles supply:

•   A first Left Brain Overview. You've come back across the corpus callosum, Right Brain to Left Brain. The Left Brain has the job of decoding the Right Brain's image-speak. Which is the ideal role for the Left Brain to adopt in all matters related to creativity.

•   A current focus. What you think this story is about at this moment. If it stays the same, all well and good. If it changes, it'll alert you early on to the change which can be extraordinarily helpful. When a writer is deep-into-process, a loss of focus often occurs. That loss of focus the writer may not be aware of for quite a while unless the Working Title is in place to nudge, remind and stare at you from the top of the page.

• An informative comparison. A later changed Working Title allows you to keep track of the writing process. You can look back and see how your ideas developed. What factors influenced those changes and developments. These fine distinctions inbuild a better Right Brain/Left Brain connection, and move a writer towards more integrated whole brain functioning.

• The seeding of good habits. Like most beginner-writers, I initially ignored the Working Title advice. Now I recognise the Working Title's great contribution to the overall developmental process. The Working Title focuses your mind and acts to remove woolly thinking, so takes your idea forward another stage.

• An essence of your piece as of now. The length of the working title is immaterial. Don't let a certain unwieldiness of expression be a reason not to give a piece a working title.

Example of four Action Images producing a storyline

Two Action Images were used as they are and two were adapted to suit the emerging storyline.

Storyline - Working title – Flying Flowers

The two Action Images used in their original form are:

> *A hearse pursued by the police, doing eighty down a motorway, flowers flying off its roof.*
> *Paper boy walking across waste ground.*

The two adapted Action Images are:

Flowers move on a pond but there is no wind. This was changed to goldfish behaving strangely in the pond and their lady owner seeking the vet's advice.

*During church service, the Reverend Soames finds the water turned into wine. This was changed to the Reverend **hallucinating** the water being turned into wine.*

Questions beginning *'what if...'* prompted the development of the following rough story line from these four Action Images.

Rough storyline of 'Flying Flowers'

1   The hearse doing eighty mph down the motorway. The driver is a drug runner late for an assignment.

2   Possibly late because of a girlfriend (backstory). Coffin contains new illegal drugs.

3   The police let the driver off with a warning, not suspecting anything amiss.

4   The flowers that flew off in the chase have been kept with the drugs. The drugs acts on the flowers in a contaminating way.

5   Some scattered flowers end up in a pond, some on waste ground.

6   Goldfish in the pond behave strangely, start jumping. The old lady who owns the pond and goldfish calls the vet.

7   The vet finds fish drugged and reports it to the police.

8   The old lady is questioned, her garden searched. Police discover a cache of arms.

9   The old lady's son buried them there (backstory) unknown to the old lady.

10   Son and old lady have fallen out.

11   The flowers blown onto the waste ground are sniffed by a newspaper boy, who gets high.

12   He quickly involves his friends, they collect and preserve the flowers.

13   Local bees (in the garden next to the pond) produce drugged honey.

14   The effect of the drug is intensified – made more potent - through the pollen from the drugged flowers being processed by the bees into honey.

15   Badgers who steal the beekeeper's honey from hives so like it they storm the catflap to get more.

16   Some honey is sold to the vicar. During Sunday sermon, the vicar hallucinates, believes the water's turned to wine and declares a miracle.

Overview on storyline of Flying Flowers

Honey, the sale of it, could open the story to novel length in terms of the different ways the drug, taken through the honey, affects people.

So the situation is:

The real culprit, the drug runner, has escaped.

Everyone who eats the honey is in trouble. Beekeeper, old lady, vicar.

The paperboy is in deep trouble because his pre-served flowers are quite lethal.

The police will be taken in the wrong direction twice which opens up a range of further 'wrong connections'.

It is Interrogation of Image for story-making that promotes an excellent Right Brain/Left Brain creative relationship. Asking questions of characters and situations is taken to another – *wholistic** – level if it is an *image* rather than a *concept* which is being related to and/or interrogated.

Analysis and Interrogation

There is a potential confusion of terms here.

Analysis examines what is present, takes it apart for the purpose of seeing how it's made up and works. Analysis is like a closed system that has no outside references except those which illuminate meaning already present. Left Brain convergence is its driver.

Interrogation in a creative context also examines what is present, but for a different purpose. To see what is there that can grow, imaginatively, and 'come alive' for writer and reader alike. Growth of story material through interrogation of image is the goal. Interrogation is like an open system which is continuously looking to expand and deepen its parameters. Right Brain divergence is its driver.

Different levels and types of questions

Interrogation of image or story material comes at different levels, according to what aspect the writer wishes to develop. What motivates the questions in the first place. Is it to learn more about a character? Is it to produce a great plot? Is it to write a long work that has great universality – a novel that speaks to and touches many people? From a writer's viewpoint, it's helpful to distinguish three areas of questioning. These three areas are:

1   Closed-ended questions
2   Questions that remain questions for a while
3   Questions expansive of story material

1 Closed-ended questions

These are the kind of questions that inform a character profile. Name, age, height, weight, job or career, likes, dislikes, hobbies, ambitions, weaknesses, strengths. The more you know about the character, the more real and alive s/he'll feel to you. This is the *relational* aspect of Right Brain functioning, and the reason role-playing your characters is so effective. You can do character profiles in tick-box style, but factor in you may need to change some aspects as you get to know them better.

2 Questions that remain questions for a while

For a writer characters grow. It's incremental, a real 'getting-to-know-them' process. Questions that remain questions are valid. The fact you have asked the question, even though you haven't a clue about the answer, is good enough. You need to build a tolerance for unanswered questions because they are part of that 'messy process' of creativity which will resolve itself given time, and a little patience.

3 Questions expansive of story

These questions are ones which may arise naturally in the course of organic development of story material a writer feels passionate about. It's a good way to check out an idea's growth potential on a large canvas *before* you invest too much time and energy in a project that, as David Campton, the most prolific stage playwright in the U.K. said, 'hasn't the legs to run'.

1   *Follow the dream!*
        Indeed, how could any writer *not* look at a story-idea in relation to themselves! Yet it's possible to go further and ask some tangential questions. How does this idea relate to something that's happened to me? How does it relate to something I have done or wanted to do in my life? What unfulfilled desire in my life has led to this idea? By probing a little deeper, you may discover a richness of understanding and connection you were not conscious of previously.

2   *Myth / fairy tale / legend*

Continue this same type of aslant questioning. By so doing, you may hit upon exactly the right question to ask at that moment, and simultaneously discover the deep power of interrogation as integral to process. E.g. What myth, fairy tale or legend relates to this idea? Does it have any relevance for me? If it doesn't, the writing might lack necessary power. If my story is a modern reinvention, how can I translate that myth into contemporary terms? Are there several myths buried in this idea? If so, which myth is dominant?

3   *The zeitgeist or current world concerns*

How does my idea relate to concerns which are uppermost in the world at the moment? Be they political, social, economic, fashion, whatever. What way can I link my idea to that to develop a story?

4   *Reinvention, reversals of any 'same old' aspects*

The story implicit in a seed-idea may well have been done before. Redoing it, swopping contemporary for historical, comedic for tragic and employing all manner of reversals can be exciting.

5   *Tone/treatment*

What tone is coming from this? Is it funny, tragic, serious, skittish, send-up, heroic, streetwise? Obviously this depends on the writer's treatment of the idea, but there are many options.

6   *Issues*

The story idea may well imply a question. E.g.: About H.I.V., women's rights, environmentalism. Ask yourself the question directly, '*What do I think about this issue?*' It will inform the story, often developing it with great power. However, if the writer finds it hard to dissociate from self-generated material because it is so personally meaningful, the danger is the move towards propaganda. This is where the advice to 'distribute your personal views over all your characters' is important to stop your main character from becoming your mouthpiece. To take the opposite point of view is, strategically, a good move.

It confronts the writer with the dilemmas – both personal ones and those inherent in the issue. An added bonus is it makes for more interesting, subtle and stronger writing.

7   *The human condition*

This is advice to find shared commonality of experience that ensures your readers empathise – and don't just sympathise – with your characters' predicaments. The 'we've all been there' moments presented obliquely acts as both hook and refresh.

8   *God / power*

'What part does God play in this idea?' It can be whatever God you like, but the idea of Man against God is a theme which has been running through literature for the last three thousand years. Nor need it be religious. God, after all, can be one's employer.

Another way to look at this one is 'What power relationships are implicit in this idea?'

9   *Territory*

Related to power is the subject of territory, the defence or taking of territory. That is, a bit of the earth's surface, big or small. Again, territory is a big theme through literature and one that writers return to, again and again. We live in a crowded world and our little bit of space is important to every one of us. Whether that space it is real or metaphoric space.

10   *Alienation / dislocation*

What degree of alienation, in whatever terms, might be present in this idea? There's a tendency to see aliens, these days, in terms of creatures from other planets. In contemporary terms, the expression *aliens* can be applied quite comfortably to any minority group, including writers.

11   *Journey*

Unlike the headings above, journey does have structural implications for a story. 'Journey' doesn't necessarily mean a physical journey, it can be a metaphorical one. (See Chapter 17).

People are often told in writing seminars that there

must be some change in the main character's circumstances or state of mind, even in the shortest story. The main point to remember concerning journey is to ensure your *readers* go on one.

12   *Significance*

The seed idea may be about nothing which is intrinsically important. Story judges call them the 'so what?' stories. The sense, when you reach the end, the feeling you are left with is 'so what?' Personal stories that have no universal qualities about them at all – do nothing to reach out to the reader – come into this category. The recommendation to 'never forget your reader' breathes new life into a story that's in danger of becoming a 'so-what?' story.

Put story material through this 12 point expansion process and it will be easier to answer the defining and focusing question... 'What is this story about?' or 'What *might* this story be about?' A multiplicity of answers ensures you have a richness which gives universality, but try to find one statement that expresses the heart and passion.

A worked example of expansive questions applied to the storyline of 'Flying Flowers'

1 Follow the dream.

Flowers are short lived, very beautiful, nature's quintessence. They are:

- symbols of peace and love,
- sexual stage before fruit,
- colourful,
- ephemeral.

The smell of these drugged flowers is unusual, other - worldly, a sense of the forbidden leading to the realism of specific hallucinations in story characters. Pollen into honey seeds the idea of metamorphosis – a fundamental altering of character which echoes the story characters' predicament.

2 Myth / fairy tale / legend.

Flowers are an integral part of many celebrations. A flower behind the ear in Hawaii is a sign of availability. Flowers pass between people as tokens. Their symbolism is woven deep into human relationships. Seeds on the wind - or drugged flowers in this case - give the story a sense of how things happen by chance.

Every flower carries a symbology in myth, legend or saga, e.g. Hawthorn and Glastonbury in Celtic or Druidic legend. Funeral wreaths contain different flowers according to time of year, and (sometimes) the deceased's wishes. The backstory here could be the deceased cultivated a flower with particular properties and insisted on its presence at his funeral, knowing the likely outcome; revenge on the world without having to meet the consequences. Revenge is a powerful motivator in story.

3   World concerns.

'What if-ing' the story here leads to follow-up questions. Do the drugged flowers have properties other than hallucinatory? Water into wine indicates that people think their hallucinations are real, as with L S D, so one effect of the drug is to alter the sense of taste and smell. Does whoever sniffs these flowers begin to inhabit a different world of senses, for instance, an animal world of senses? Authorities, worldwide, attempt to crack down on drugs; while other people make a lot of money selling drugs. A story development could be someone gets hold of the flowers with a view to replication and making money. For example, the paperboy's elder brother sees the commercial possibilities and shrewdly sets up his younger brother to carry the blame. (This is an example of 'turning the screws' on your character.)

4   Reinvention

There is an echo of various Greek mythology stories involving the sirens luring heroes onto rocks. Jason and Odysseus were both tested this way. As in 'if you get too close, you lose control of the situation and can do nothing about it'. This is the paperboy's situation, but all who eat the drugged honey will feel this too. To the logical mind, it may seem a huge jump from an ancient myth from another culture to a modern contemporary story, but many highly successful novels and films are, when stripped to the theme, clearly reinventions.

5   Tone / treatment

This story lends itself to a combination of the humorous and sinister, or simply humorous, or solely sinister. It could be a mystery, a thriller, a combination, a serious piece about a new drug and its effects on people for good or ill. This story has high degrees of irony and paradox, and the potential for cruel twists of fate for the paperboy.

6   What do I think about this issue?

Drugs are higher profile than when this storyline was first invented. Personally, I don't have strong feelings about this issue, except the tendency towards over-reliance on drugs generally. With Flying Flowers, the vulnerability and manipulative issues back of the storyline are of far more personal interest, alongside its humorous potential.

7   The human condition

The human condition where people enter other mind-states can be highly productive. To bring out that aspect helps balance any whitewashing perspective concerning drugs. The fact that the characters who are experiencing the effects of these drugs have not willingly taken them and that they are neither recreational nor prescribed, alters their position and makes them victims.

8   God / power

Power is in the flowers and the people who find out what's in the flowers. It is then taken to the next level by the characters themselves. Where the vicar interprets his experience as God-given, the paperboy's elder brother is prepared to sacrifice his sibling for financial gain.

9   Territory

How far have these flowers gone? Where have the seeds drifted to, if any of these flowers get to seed. (Which they will, of course, because that fulfils another story requirement – increasing, not just the tension, but the story's power, significance and ultimately reader involvement by simply making things a lot worse than originally assumed, but doing this in ways totally believable.)

This could have implications for a twist-ending, or a second wave, where a second generation of flowers evolve and produce entirely new effects and problems.

10   Alienation / dislocation

A sense of personal dislocation is a permanent part of this story from the individual characters' perspectives. The normalcy of slightly backward English village life - church, vicar, eccentricities of the old lady, W.I. centred community - act as a counterbalance. This background to the story offers humorous counterpoint.

11   Journey

The individual characters' story journeys will be unique because the way the drug affects people is different in all cases. This attribute will delay the piecing together of the full picture, because commonality of experience will not be present to encourage people to make the right connections.

12   Significance

The drug could have beneficial effects when refined and rid of its toxic elements. In its unrefined state, the drug has both positive and negative qualities, and the negative properties are stronger. One possible significant outcome of this story is the place of drugs in relation to mankind in the future.

What is this story about?

This is the focusing question for the writer, It is clear, from the twelve questions asked of the original Action Image, Flying Flowers is a story that could go in many directions, according to the choices made by the writer who developed it. It is not linear, it is multi-faceted. Its richness, significance and meaningfulness in larger contexts is evident through this 12 point expansion process.

Let us stay with what Flying Flowers might be about.

Flying Flowers might be about...

1   Thematically, how an innocent innocuous act can lead a person (here, the paperboy) down a path from which there is no return.

2   Opportunistic behaviour as a modern culture driver. The paperboy's brother's journey, echoed in the drug runner's.

3   How the human relationship with nature – through drug development - mirrors evolution. A *wholistic** appreciation.

4   How surface appearances can be a force to hide 'what's really going on'. This may be an 'agenda-based' take or a genuine unknowing. In this story, both forces operate.

5   How people wrongly interpret an 'unknown' within the framework of their belief system. A 'restricted thinking' perception which the *Reverend Soames'* story, if used, would reveal both humorously and clearly.

6   The unpredictable element in life which results from a lack of care. (The situation we all share, the real universality.)

7   One person seeding a force for evil in the world as an act of revenge on the next generation. Due to the ingenuity of the people involved, this is eventually turned around.

This worked example demonstrates that coming at your story-material from many different angles but still keeping the parameters wide, opens up its potential to universality – those things all human beings share. It also reveals more of the fullness of possibility in terms of both character and plot development. It's often said that a story needs to work at seven levels. Self-generated Action Images backed up by a series of expansive questions leads to such a multi-layered appreciation.

Ways into creative technique

This is where you take over. The goal is to make this process work for you, not tick boxes.

After reading this chapter you may feel overwhelmed by choice. This is a real possibility because the 12 subheads represent alternative ways forward. To use any one as leader and use others in support-roles for what you want to say influences the development of an idea. It gives slant, bias, angle, emphasis and ultimately colours its treatment to make the development unique, stamped with your Writer's Voice.

This last exercise offers a way to refocus.

Draw a mindmap of what personally inspires you. Go wide. Trawl your life for early inspiration. Develop a sensitivity and acuity for things you are attracted to or drawn to. Then consider how these deep motivators might power your writing.

Inspiration is often talked about as if it's an entity that arrives from outer space and happens to target your head. This is not a useful way to understand inspiration. It has too much in common with the public image of a writer sitting around 'waiting to be inspired'. Inspiration has thousands of sources.

Here's just three - in overview form.

1   The felt-sense of breakthrough into something completely new.

2   A coming together (synthesis) in an extraordinary but nevertheless personally valid, powerful and real way.

3   The experience of something never before seen, dreamed of or witnessed. This experience affects you so strongly it causes a personal paradigm shift of such magnitude you know you will never see the world in quite the same way again.

These three overviews offer more useful ways to contact inspiration and, more importantly, *re-contact* it later to give energy, passion, fire, exuberance, enthusiasm and wit to your writing. The whole range of human highs with their sense of expanded consciousness and tremendously alive states is just the kind of inspiration that writers need.

Though you may look outside for inspiration, and find it, a time may come when your personal inner inspirers clamour for attention. Imagine that time has come right now. Reconsider the record you now have in your Learning Journal. Are there some places where inspiration was particularly high and can be concretised on that 0 to 10 scale? Can you pinpoint the connectors? Say why the images, visualisations or exercises worked - or didn't work - for you? By reaching this level of self-knowing you will develop a less fickle and more reliable relationship with inspiration. To develop an active working relationship with inspiration is to ground your writing in the best way possible, into the passion of your life.

17 Informative Overviews & Ongoing Learning

Writers need the ability to communicate a fullness of expression. With its sense-based remit, Right Brain work generally takes them in that direction. Writers also need the opposite quality – a facility to condense and define, or distil, essences. Fortunately the two – fullness of expression and an ability to condense – are complementary, found in the same place, the Right Brain.

It's easier to say an image's meaning in a sentence – or a range of sentences all with a different angle or take – than it is to work from a complicated and complex concept. That's the time when words become traps that take writers into verbose, unwieldy, longwinded, extended sentences that accurately reflect the befuddlement of over intellectualism or too much Left Brain work generally. In real life, we meet it in administrator-jargon, where clarity of meaning has long ago departed.

Right Brain qualities imaged

Just to refresh your memory, those twenty Right Brain attributes are:

Images & symbols: creative: visual: concrete: wholistic*: intuitive: random: synthesising: relational: divergent: non-linear: simultaneous: infinitive: imagination rules: big picture oriented: looks at wholes: colour: subjective: risk-taking: sense-based.

Draw them with the remit of individualising them and the new perceptions that emerge are directly translatable into Left Brain appreciations and important writer skills.

'*Looks at wholes*' alerts us to the fragmenting and fragmentary nature of much of daily human life. The compartmentalised frameworks on our modern daily lives means we may lose any sense of it being 'all joined up'.

For the writer, drawing lots of 'wholes' around the words on the page, in different sizes and colours, offers further appreciations. Each aspect of your writing project is one whole. Your task is to fit them all together and *get the balance right.* Gazing at a group of random and colourful wholes drawn on a single page is a reminder to look at a piece of work with an eye to this balance. Is there a need to emphasise, or de-emphasise anywhere? Or, in Right Brain language, to blow up or shrink the size of some of the wholes in the interests of the major thrust and focus of your work? Or, in kinaesthetic language, which draws on the felt-sense of Right Brain functioning, is there an over-weighting of one section and is another too light and needs further development?

'Big picture oriented' is a reminder that we often do think too small, in contexts ranging from the personal to the global. 'Big picture oriented' is a concrete image too, easy to imagine and draw. The idea of many pictures, as personal worldviews, both disabling and empowering, spawned the psychological system of 'reframing' (NLP) so has great credibility.

'Big picture oriented' is also the view from the plane, with the whole landscape laid out below you in two-dimensional patterns. So you can clearly see the lie of the (mind)-land and how things fit together – structurally or fictionally. For writers, this is a major skill to access and draw on in putting together a clear and coherent piece of work, whether fiction or non-fiction.

One skill that eludes many writers is organisation of material, especially if it is a lot of material. A distancing is necessary and that distancing is often referred to imaginatively as 'the need to get above your subject'. New writers struggle to gain this perspective on their work unless they already have acquired this skill through other channels, such as meditation.

The Nation of Images

The words *Image* and *imagination* have more in common than the first two syllables.

This word we use for human creativity at its height – without too much of a stretch of the imagination – re-presents itself as 'Nation of Images'.

If we follow that line of thought we may reach the surprising conclusion that imagination is simply the Nation of Images available to each and every one of us courtesy of our Right Brains.

This personal Nation of Images is the source and home of your individual creativity and your individual infinite well of creativity and thus deserves deep respect. If you give inner imagery this deep respect, it will reward you in ways you cannot at present imagine or predict.

You can sense and savour inner imagery's power. It is a personal empowerment route open to all writers who wish to deepen their creativity and improve their connections to a personal infinite well of creativity. Writing from that creative power source gives authenticity and strength.

Demand it; expect it and it may desert. Honour its particular ways of expression that are unique to you. Get to know them intimately, particularly the *patterns* behind the new forms you create. This is the writer's work and joy, by turns frustrating and utterly absorbing. Acknowledge the negative emotions by all means, but learn the many ways to bypass those that block personal creativity.

By using these strategies you will keep the creative juices flowing and not complain about the drought where there's just a trickle or the flood when the imaginative damn bursts and the process goes temporarily out of control. Acceptance takes you forward quicker than any other attitude.

If it really is a Nation of Inner Images we individually possess, then the idea it's an infinite resource we can draw on feels right, normal and natural. Push the metaphor one stage further, and we take the Right Brain/Left Brain dialogue to a new level. Self-development gurus have been saying much the same thing for fifty or more years. When Left Brain dominates and Right Brain is suppressed, we close down our creativity. When Right Brain is leader and allowed to stay in that position in all matters creative, we recognise this priceless gift as one truly ours.

Our human brain functioning is basically the same. To discuss human brain functioning as if it were a personality issue, a belief issue, an upbringing issue or even a gender issue superimposes wrong frameworks that stop us seeing the larger picture. Of course any one person's Right Brain/Left Brain functioning is utterly unique. We see this in that individuality of style that hallmarks those people who choose to become writers. The main thing is to ensure its effects, overall, are expansive and satisfying, not restrictive and silencing.

The larger picture

Several centuries ago, the U.K. population endured a highly repressive regime due to the existence of two alternative branches of Christianity – Catholicism and Protestantism. The fundamental difference between these two religions did not concern the god they worshipped. It was supposed to be the same god. True, the Goddess aspect was more in evidence in Catholicism through the veneration of the Virgin Mary. The main difference concerned images – richly present in Catholicism, minimal in Protestantism. At its root, the issue tearing the country apart and the cause of massive bloodshed concerned the presence or absence of *images!*

The uncertainty surrounding the role of images in our lives has been around a long time. The fact images formed the focus of religious warfare suggests that their power on and over people was recognised even then. Fortunately, today we can turn that knowledge of the power of image to good use – to forward our own art of writing.

Metaphor's larger picture

Metaphor is the nearest that language comes to image-speak. Metaphor stands at the cross-over point for writers because of its image-base. But the implication is always that language is the superior communicator. At the surface level – instructions, basic information, - this is true. A*ll the 'yes, no, turn right at the next junction and it's hundred yards on your left, the meeting is at 11a.m. sharp, food's on the table'* language comes into this category. Though sign-language is often as good, a nod, a shake of the head, the hand pointing, or going through a series of arm-moves.

This book is about using the part of our brains that, historically, intellectually, has less credibility in western culture. This applies particularly, as well as generally, to the person who is a non-artist. It's my hope that this book helps to reframe that perception for those artists called writers.

Images for this book

Two images informed this book. The first was 'a tight weave'. This concerned the organisational structure of the book. Yet the experience of writing it and rereading it speaks to me more of 'journey'. Both 'a tight weave' and 'journey' inform its structure. 'A tight weave' is the organisational imperative; 'the journey' the experiential, incorporating Right Brain feeling-states. They are complementary images.

A tight weave – the initial informing metaphor for this book

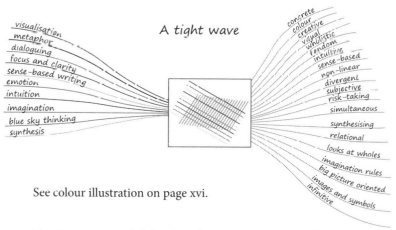

See colour illustration on page xvi.

This is my personal debrief on the appropriateness of this image for the structural development of this book.

1   Not an image that attracted me initially, nevertheless I felt and understood its sense of rightness for the book.

2   Indicates a need to pay attention to tightness. Not as in verboseness v. succinctness of style, but the fine weave. To focus on the connection of fine weave with refinement.

3   It worked out as a need to go back time and again to attend to that weave.

4   As a creative person, I 'thought-jump' a lot. It's not just a question of slowing down because if it was the job would be easy. It's more a need to 'tease apart' what is already there to insert another fine thread that will make the overall picture even clearer.

5   At first I was concerned and focused on warp and weft – the crossovers between creativity and writing... their interweaving and meeting points. This occupied all my thoughts, and yet it wasn't until I began 'inserting further fine strands' that this book really started to come together.

6   From the outset 'further fine strands' was a Right Brain image that repeatedly nudged me, asserting its importance. Yet for a couple of months I didn't see fully how to translate 'further fine strands' into the process of writing the book.

7   It wasn't until I finally related to the image's meaning at a dynamic level – that 'teasing apart' quality - that I broke through.

8   When I consider what I have learned, the following emerged. I didn't integrate the image, or stay with it, or contemplate it long enough at the start. I didn't work through how it would translate into the daily business of planning and writing. I let its 'not very attractive' impression (subjective evaluation) just put me off a little, so the absolute rightness of the image-to-book link took longer to emerge.

But there was more to follow. Towards the end of writing this book, a further four meanings emerged for me. At the time I wasn't thinking about a tight weave as the defining overview for this book. These meanings just jumped into my mind, unbidden. To me this impromptu arrival illustrates extraordinarily well how the Right Brain functions - at its own pace and in its own way. The precision of meaning to be derived from an inner image can be astonishing.

1   The rectangular. The tight weave I always envisaged as a rectangle, not a square. Now it occurred to me how precise this image was. It gives the warp of ten key Writer Skills and the weft of twenty Right Brain functions that serve the writer.

2   The Right Angles. All the right angles made between warp and weft are direct meeting and *re-meeting points*. It's possible to pick any point in the weave and trace it back two ways - to Writer Skill and Right Brain. This is easy enough to do visually. Doing it via words and concepts takes a whole book.

3   The Plot-Weave. A plot-weave is a shorthand way of embodying - as in give substance to and so embody - the dynamic matrix of event and character that is the warp and weft of story.

4   The power of attractive v. unattractiveness. I've referred to this a number of times, because it is so often the basis of human decision-making. Here it gets a final airing

How we personally bypass a feeling of dislike - or even an emotional neutrality-towards an inner image is an important consideration. One thing is certain. We need to value the image over the initial emotional response if we are not to depower our own inner images! Here lies a subtle form of self-sabotage!

Journey – experiential metaphor for this book

This book is also a journey, where journey functions as a metaphor for all that happens on a physical journey to a new place. Here's 9 ways this book is a journey

1   It's expansive. It opens up the world (inner world) in a way rarely seen or appreciated.

2   On the way, you pass places where the gut-reaction is *"That looks interesting. I wouldn't mind visiting there sometime.'*

3   Preconceptions get knocked or are challenged. *'I didn't think it would be like that!'* Well, what did you think it'd be like? Whether said in delight or disappointment is also important.

4   All the outer visuals of a journey affect us, alter our mindstate. We arrive in the new place in a frame of mind quite unlike the one we were in at the outset.

5   If we break the journey at different places – do the interactive within the chapters – we make personally interesting discoveries.

6   The newness and fresh experience is stimulating in itself, especially if imagery and imagework is mainly unexplored mind territory.

7   Landmarks, identified on the way, tweak memories. Social history, battles, archaeology, famous people who lived and worked in places travelled through. Maybe we want to

connect with them for a while. It's often the sole reason people take a particular journey.

8 The way itself – whether a British motorway, winding lane, outback dust track, ocean crossing, - takes you forward. The 'moved-on' sense within journeying is strong.

9 The arrival, does it offer you what you hoped, or are your sights already on another destination, more appropriate for you? Questions, remember, can ultimately be quite as useful as answers. Consider questions, whether self-questions or the interrogation of writing material, as way-stations in the thinking process that leads to new insights, little revelations, or unexpected connections. Prepare the way, open the mind, don't cut off.

Further ways into Image

Personalised imaging of Right Brain qualities
This is a different take on the perennial advice to writers to have a notice prominently displayed in large letters in their writing space... 'Make a scene of it!' Instead, (or as well as), create personalised images of the 20 Right Brain functions and decorate the walls of your workspace with them. Not only will it help you to 'make a scene of it', it will also remind you of the many other Right Brain qualities that are so useful to writers.

The journey metaphor
Use the journey metaphor to record in your Learning Journal the following.

What's been the most interesting and useful fact of the journey through this book. That singular perception underlies an important writer skill, the ability to condense into a single sentence.

What's the best personal experience of all the ways you encountered or chose to explore? And why does it stand out?

Alternative route
If it wasn't a journey – metaphorically – find an image that says it as it is for you. Remember, it is in the imaginative need to go beyond what was presented or shown to us, that the personally

creative is located. Skydive, sea-dive, rocket launch, takes journey into other areas. Develop – play with - the facility to ground emotion and feeling-states into metaphors. This is metaphor functioning as modern shorthand to instantly communicate the whole experience to listener or reader. It grounds an idea in an image which has a solidity. (Is concrete, Right Brain.) Compared to an idea which can be easily be lost if vague, ephemeral.

Second alternative route

Growth, particularly imaginative growth, closely mirrors organic growth. It's a process of continual splitting and parting of the ways. Often enough, a journey starts by being one thing and changes (metamorphoses) into something else en route. This isn't a simplistic bad/good polarity or anything oppositional. It's a way of relating (relational is Right Brain) to experience which illuminates the subjective (individual appreciation) and so makes it personally meaningful. The invitation here is to explore, in a playful yet curious way, the feeling-states and experience of the journey through a book. It doesn't have to be this book. Another one may spring to mind that'd better fit your creative purpose. For the sake of your writing, remember to make it a Right Brain one.

18   Re-imaging

A writer's evolution

The beginner asks *'Can I do it?' 'Am I capable?' 'Have I got what it takes?'*

The person who has been writing for a while asks different questions altogether, based on awareness of choice. It's just that you are at a different stage, further on in the process so have an expanded awareness of what's possible.

The more experienced writer asks:

'What is the most effective way I can do this?' 'The easiest way for the reader to grasp,' or *'the most entertaining/interesting way to show (not tell) this story'.* The frameworks have changed. This is the writer's journey.

It's an evolution. Images too display a similar tendency to evolve through time.

Reframing at the Right Brain level

This is reframing in action at the Right Brain level. It's the Right Brain's method of communicating when it realises the Left Brain hasn't quite got the whole picture. Through the fresh emphasis given to fill out the picture, an important consideration or awareness is factored in. This Right Brain nudge may do something even more important. Show the writer the whole project needs a re-evaluation from another viewpoint, through asking a slightly different question.

The writer too may initiate this process by changing the overview question, altering the focus to its ultimate high-density resolution. This is Right Brain/Left Brain working together, the whole brain partnership.

Do not be concerned if your images change. It's a sign you are moving to the next level, discerning more meaning and enriching a personal appreciation that you couldn't have 'got to' earlier because the necessary connections weren't in place. It may be a more empowering image or a complementary one that comes to you in this process of inner evolution of images. Use both. Trust the process.

It is doing what Jean Houston suggests is possible at the mega-level, the cultural level, as we discussed in Chapter 15. e.g. By changing the imagery around the subject, we change its meaning for us. It's the easiest, most natural and organic way to 'see it' differently.

A re-classification of artwork and its importance for writers

Once again, the word 'journey' is being used in the metaphorical sense. This section describes the journey of this book in a few more ways. This rich contextualisation helps embed and reinforce understanding at the *wholistic** level in a similar way as a single self-generated image offers many meanings.

Some people like classifications and categories. Some people do not, believing they restrict thinking, which they do. E.g. Much of the early part of this book is concerned with dissociating inner imagery from representational art. If you still hold the feeling that good representational artists are in a higher league or have an inbuilt advantage over non-artists when it comes to creating and using self-generated images for writing purposes, this next section is specially for you.

A good representational artist works with outer images. That's the focus. A good representational artist is unlikely to develop an interest in, or facility for, producing inner images. That's outside the representational artist's normal remit. There's nothing to stop the representational artist taking this route, if s/he wants to, of course. It's just that usually the goal is completely different.

A useful analogy is this one. We need to create a divorce, a break-up, between the association of producing self-generated images and being a good artist. One way we can do this is by a re-classification of functions. Move imagery from being the exclusive property of the artist to being the property of the writer or anyone who chooses to use it for self-development or therapy. Then the writer may wholeheartedly embrace self-generated images as a working tool of the writing profession or hobby.

It's a paradigm shift requiring a change in brainview. If seen as such, it will impress itself at an effective level.

The ideal creative relationship

The new creative marriage is between the Right Brain and the self-generated image with the Left Brain in the role of support and back-up. That's the relationship to foster and develop. This needs to be experienced at the felt-sense level, not the intellectual level. At the felt-sense level, it creates an impression that fundamentally alters attitude, behaviour and belief. It changes the thinking structure, rejigs the brainview.

Hopefully, you now have reached the stage in your thinking where you see that bringing representational art into the debate or discussion in the first place is a diversion, a wrong move, a tiresome sidetrack.

Instead, you are more than happy to reframe inner imagery as a working partner of your writing, available twenty-four/seven, literally. It's akin to laying claim to a birthright, to something that was yours when you were born.

Jill Bolte Taylor is a young brain researcher famous for her experience of watching herself have a stroke from which she subsequently made a full recovery. (en.wikipedia. org/wiki/Jill_Bolte_Taylor). Jill likens the two hemispheres of the brain as *parallel processors*. Literally, two brains in one, both entirely different, yet complementary in their functioning, so confirming the old saying 'the whole is greater than the sum of the parts'.

The more contexts you conceive this relationship between inner imagery, personal creativity and writing, the better. The more it will hold, so never again will you assign your Left Brain a creative task that is the department and province of the Right Brain to deal with and sort.

The cultural perception of artists has always been *fringe* to some extent. If we keep this classification uppermost in our minds - the standard by which we writers judge and assess - the inevitable result is that, for non-artists, imagery is pretty much a no-go area.

This book's journey can be seen as one where your relationship with art, in the form of inner imagery, may well have started as distant, passive or even non-existent. By the end of the journey, if you have given the visualisation exercises and self-generated images a go, their power will have made itself known to you. This is validation of the highest order.

Image-speak communicates so many things simultaneously, it's a smorgasbord (metaphorically) of information.

Decoding personal symbology long term

Decoding personal symbology is fun and fascinating. The personal revelations within this decoding can make you want to shout, laugh or deeply respect it. All of these reactions are heartfelt and genuine. They will lead you to the next level, where you see the flexibility of image-speak and witness how its language-base grows the more you train and use the Left Brain in its newly assigned interpretive Right Brain supportive role.

Sometimes, it needs the wake-up call of groupwork to demonstrate this. Experience, after all, is the greatest teacher. A recent 'doodling workshop' I ran took my thinking to another level.

Doodling as a primer in Imagespeak

This workshop was planned as an introduction to doodling as a Right Brian activity. My initial plan was to share the doodles produced by the writers with the goal of extending their range of doodling. To give writers who attended the session more 'doodling tools' to keep their interest high. But it changed direction mid-session and I, as facilitator of this group of writers, found myself on a steep learning curve.

Doodling is comparable to a hot-write: the permission to explore, free-associate, and go where the pen takes you. The 'nothing-on-it' quality is liberating. Of itself, the requirement to 'go further', extends the boundaries, a move so useful to the creative writer. It is in 'going further' that the writer finds things, connections, thoughts, ideas, that can literally open up a whole new world.

It is likely that, for the non-artists, drawing itself may well be put into this category of 'going further' than normal. This is just the beginning.

When a group of over thirty writers showed and shared

their doodles, I was astonished at the insights. Particularly, the individual biases and emphases that emerged in the way each person presented and *framed,* as in *contextualised* their doodling to the group. The shock for me was in seeing the direct relationship to the twenty Right Brain functions.

The focus of the session changed direction because of my gut reaction and intuitive feeling (Right Brain again) that the most important thing for writers to realise - and take away with them - was how their doodles expressed the 20 Right Brain skills listed on the handout. And to go on to see how other writers' doodles reflected a different group of Right Brain functions.

*Wholistic** naturally featured a lot, but sometimes 'divergent', 'synthesising' 'relational' or 'infinitive' led the way. With 20 skills in the frame, and an infinite number of ways of decoding possible, just hearing what individual writers say about their doodles is revelatory. Straightaway, without prior prompting or contextualising, some writers talked about their doodling in terms of the Right Brain functions - the connections came to them automatically and immediately. But many of the writers did not, and I felt it was important to be clear about the association between the freestyle drawing we know as doodling and its source in Right Brain functioning.

That way, the writers learned the range of Right Brain skills they currently favoured, and saw how other writers favoured and used another quite different set. This double appreciation, repeatedly confirming the connection, gave individuals an anchor and also an insight into Right Brain functioning generally. As normal, the images produced were disparate and had nothing in common superficially, yet the way the writers talked about their images rooted them firmly into the twenty Right Brain skills.

This session became a primer in learning imagespeak, showing the places we all talk the same - Right Brain- language.

Only one person chose to scribble, as might a bored three year old child. Scribbling reflects chaos, and chaos is often, at the felt-sense level, a sign of a high creative state.

A warning is perhaps in order here. There is no 'right or wrong' with respect to this type of investigation. To scribble madly is cathartic and this same person, in a different mood, might doodle something very different. Again, we witness a bypassing of a cultural negative, for this writer must have felt a certain permission - allowing, freedom - to risk ridicule in producing such scribbles and sharing them with the group. And, of course risk-taking itself is a Right Brain function.

The best validation for doodling comes from seeing how the doodles, when decoded by the writers themselves, accurately reflect the 20 Right Brain functions. This acts as a first glimpse into personal Right Brain functioning - something we all possess whether we choose to use it or not.

And to go one step further... Apparently, we as a species share this Right and Left Brain hemispherical division with dolphins, birds and many other animals. It is an across-species basic brain model.

Amongst this group of writers were habitual doodlers, non-doodlers, and those who used to doodle but had stopped because of cultural inhibitors. The group were quick to list these inhibitors, filling the flip-chart sheet in a matter of minutes. The most damning inhibitor of course being *a sign of an inability to concentrate.* This, as we now know, is the opposite of the reality - doodling aids concentration through whole-brain engagement. The doodling doesn't need any obvious or logical connection to what is being discussed. Its prime function is to keep both sides of the brain active. By its very nature doodling is completely random and involves no conscious thought.

The extension in understanding here is there's a cultural net against doodling which moves into perceptions such as not sophisticated, uncool, a waste of time, inattentive and being 'rude' to teacher. Whereas, in fact, it indicates the student, as with the physicist working at the cutting edge of his specialism mentioned in Chapter 8, prefers or needs to ensure the Right Brain is active. To de-taboo doodling, I gave each of the writers a new A4 file and asked them to cover it with doodles while I talked to them about the importance of Right Brain creativity to writers.

Sometimes, as happened with the students in this workshop, key understandings are incorporated, visually, into the doodles, while the lecturer / facilitator is speaking. There are no rules, just a fantastic diversity of response. It's this diversity which will be inhibited if students are given rules - a linear set of instructions to make the Left Brain's role leader rather than decoder. It is all too easy for the Left Brain to take up its usual role as leader, and this is one of the most obvious.

In understanding the balance of power constantly operating between Right Brain and Left Brain in every sphere of human activity, we can choose to put ourselves in creative mode by sourcing our work in the Right Brain.

This first Right Brain workshop alerted me to the fact I needed to listen at two levels... what the student said about the drawing, (reflecting uniqueness) and the Right Brain functions that came easiest and most naturally (reflecting the commonality).

Student speak in decoding personal symbology.

Students, while talking about their drawings, stopped, gasped and said things like...

'But now I've just seen that It's not only a bobbin but also a butterfly. The shape I've drawn, it's a giveaway. It's both bobbin and butterfly!'

Or, *'I've just seen a third meaning here, in the way I've drawn this interaction.'*

Or, *'Yes, it's a clef, and that's the main and obvious image, but the colours and the way they thicken and intertwine are actually more to do with...'*

These are the specifics. Students talking about an image they've just drawn, and discovering more meaning as they share with the group. And that discovery often impacts on students as revelation. They are startled, astonished, amazed. At such moments, their understanding and respect for their Right Brain leaps a thousandfold.

Some people might say this is 'hidden' information, but to me it's more informative of the process to talk in Right Brain language, than engage in the faintly mystical. What is going on here is a wonderful demonstration of Right Brain image-speak in action - visual, concrete, subjective, intuitive, imagina-

Writer Tip

To attain a balance, integration and interconnectedness between Uniqueness of Writer Voice and Universality of Experience - that which we can all relate to - is the goal of any writer who wishes to communicate.

tive, simultaneous, *wholistic**, synthesising, random, divergent, relational, colourful, and the rest - reflecting the personal associative network of each individual student. The surprise - and sometimes excitement at revelation and 'new connections being made' - accompanying these talks-outs on image and decoding personal symbology is both energising and electrifying.

A saying I find less than helpful is 'If it works, just do it'. Never mind why it works. I've always wanted to know why and often been quite sure there must be a sound reason. Don't stop at the surprise. There are two good reasons for the surprise.

1   The student wasn't previously aware of multi-meanings at the conscious level because it's information held in the Right Brain which can be accessed easily by doing imagework. And this is the same for us all!

2   There's a big range of cultural inhibitors against doing imagework.

Risk-taking too, is a Right Brain function, not one approved by the Left Brain. (Think of the hundreds of societal strictures to do with common sense, being sensible, not wasting time or 'rocking any boats'.) Over time, further blocks will emerge against doing imagework, especially if wrongly contextualised. Don't let any of them stop you!

Paradoxically, it's the multi-meanings themselves, their simultaneous appearance, that may stop a more timid writer. (Fear narrows our perceived range of options and behaviour. It's a survival strategy but has this downside.) Also, the writer may fall into the trap of wondering *'Which one is right, when the interpretations are all so different?'* i.e. random. The truth, of course is *all* are right, at some level. And this is where the subtextual emerges from that dual listening.

Decoding personal symbology in a group situation does two things.

It develops awareness of personal Right Brain functioning.

It exponentially increases awareness of Right Brain functioning generally, through listening to other students decode their work in unexpected ways.

This dual appreciation (of the decoding of their own work) coupled to the big extension such a group produces ultimately expands the overall brainview. *This is why it's a paradigm shift. Writers are primed, at a brain-based level, to produce writing conceived from a far richer context.* In a word, more *wholistic**. In the doing, more creative. Right Brain writers have more anchors into their own process and will therefore write from a stronger sense of themselves. That stronger sense is, of course, traditionally called empowerment.

In practical terms, such writers will welcome and be open to sub-textual opportunities in story-making. Subtext will not appear to them as something alien, an add-on, a literary requirement, but will be present and integrated from the start. Because the start is where it first shows itself in the drawing and image-making. The way a project naturally develops will be from this *wholistic** base because the image and its decoding gave them this dual perception. It's a form of Mastery Learning.

The trap to avoid - and there are pitfalls in plenty awaiting those who wrongly contextualise - is to attribute these breakthroughs to the 'energy of the moment', or in any way consider them as a one-off. It is possible to reconnect to the appropriate mindstate by bringing to your work the same range of qualities: open mind, expectation of something good and substantive coming from full engagement with image-making and subsequent writing, a frisson of excitement at inner-world exploration, whatever genre, style or format it takes. *Right Brain based writing leads to whole brain functioning.* At the mantric level, this is the point to grasp.

An old belief is that teachers learn more than their pupils and that is still my experience today. This is not said in humility but with delight. Of course if students independently take on, extend and develop a teacher's input, go on to magnify it back to the teacher in a completely individualistic and unexpected way, this validates the working method at its core, centre and heart. That is my felt-sense appreciation.

Consciously build your tolerance for natural Right Brain functioning. Don't linearise or impose a Left Brain orientation. Keep reminding yourself, at the mantric level...

In matters creative, the roles are reversed. Right Brain is master, Left Brain is servant.

Re-imaging self-generated images

Images aren't just self-generated images. They are *informing* images, *defining* images, *evolving* images, *working* images, *action* images, *dynamic* images! They are what your intuition tells you they are and these further fine distinctions will lead to an even deeper understanding and awareness of how much information they hold.

Ask a child to tell you what a rather unusual drawing means and the reply is often instant and surprising. Decoding personal symbology happens intuitively when we are young. Learning to decode personal symbology is not a taught subject. Nor should it be. Books on dream interpretation have already biased people towards over-reliance on outside opinion concerning their inner imagery. It's time to take back that responsibility and get our whole brain on board. How the human brain functions is the defining mega overview, regardless of any cultural perception or Left Brain bias. Working with that is the challenge. It's our natural birthright both as writers and explorers of personal creativity.

Good luck and enjoy the inner adventure!

Further reading and reference

Julia Cameron, *The Artists' Way* (G.P. Putnam's Sons 1997)

Julia Cameron, *The Vein of Gold* (G.P. Putnam's Sons 1996)

Adriana Diaz, *Freeing the Creative Spirit - Drawing on the Power of Art to tap the magic and wisdom within* (HarperSanFrancisco 1992)

Wally Caruana, *Aboriginal Art* (Thames & Hudson 1993)

Michell Cassou & Stewart Cubley, *Life, Paint and Passion - Reclaiming the magic of spontaneous expression* (G.P. Putnam's Sons 1995)

Tonya Foster and Kristin Prevallet, ed. *Third Mind: Creative Writing through Visual Art* (Teachers & Writers Collaborative 2002)

Patricia Garfield, *Creative Dreaming* (Ballantine Books 1974)

Dina Glouberman, *Life Choices & Life Changes through Imagework* (Unwin Paperbacks 1989)

Jean Houston, *The Possible Human* (Jeremy P. Tarcher/Putnam 1997)

Jean Houston, *A Mythic Life: Learning to Live Our Greater Story* (HarperSanFrancisco 1996)

Henriette Anne Klauser, *Writing on both sides of the brain* (HarperCollins 1987)

Peter London, *No More Secondhand Art - Awakening the Artist Within* (Shambhala 1989)

Nancy Margulies, *Mapping Inner Space - Learning & Teaching Visual Mapping* (Zephyr Press 2002)

Christian McEwen & Mark Statman, ed. *The Alphabet of the Trees - a Guide to Nature Writing* (Teachers & Writers Collaborative 2000)

Dave Meier, *The Accelerated Learning Handbook*
(McGraw-Hill 2000)

Candace Pert, *Molecules of Emotion - The Science Behind Mind-Body Medicine* (Simon & Shuster 1997)

Colin Rose, *Accelerated Learning*
(Accelerated Learning Systems Ltd. England 2007)

Index